GUARDED FROM ABOVE

GUARDED

FROM

ABOVE

*A Talmud Student Soldier's Account
of Miracles During World War II*

Rav Grainom Lazewnik

Translated by
Boruch M. Lazewnik

Reformatted, with explanatory footnotes by D. Z. Schwartz

A. ZEHU PUBLICATIONS

BROOKLYN

Originally titled, Persumei Nesei.
Personal Miracles: the Guiding Hand of Providence

Originally published in Hebrew as an appendix to "The Commentary of Rabbi Isaac
of Narbonne on the Alfasi, Tractate Chullin," edited from a manuscript
by Rabbi Grainom Lazewnik.
Machon Yerusholayim, 5749.

Interior and cover design by Richard Ljoenes Design LLC

Jacket photograph of the ruins of Berlin by William Vandivert

Footnotes and reformatting copyright 2022 A. Zehu Publications

Second printing, September 2024.

The publisher extends thanks to Rav Avraham Lazewnik for his kind encouragement
and generous time providing edits to the publisher's footnotes.

ISBN 979-8-9859317-0-9

For more information about this book or other titles please visit us online at
www.azehupublications.com.

A. Zehu Publications
Brooklyn

CONTENTS

GUARDED FROM ABOVE

I will proclaim Your name
to my brothers, in the midst of
the congregation I will praise You.

TEHILLIM 22.23[1]

And you shall remember
the entire journey.

DEVARIM 8.2[2]

---

1 אֲסַפְּרָה שִׁמְךָ לְאֶחָי, בְּתוֹךְ קָהָל אֲהַלְלֶךָ

2 וְזָכַרְתָּ אֶת־כָּל־הַדֶּרֶךְ

1.

INTRODUCTION

O UR SAGES MADE A CONCERTED EFFORT TO publicize and perpetuate miraculous occurrences. Holidays were established to commemorate miraculous situations and times. A special blessing of thanksgiving was instituted. Whether the miracle occurred to someone personally or to the Jewish people as a whole, a blessing may be said when visiting the location where the miracle took place.

The term "miracle" suggests the supernatural; an occurrence that is an exception to the standard patterns of our world's continuity.

There are also miracles that "occur within the continuous natural order of the world that Hashem prepares for a specific moment . . . although there was no deviance from the natural order, still, a miracle took place that Hashem prepared for this specific moment." (Mishnah Berurah and Be'ur Halacha, chapter 218 note 9, under "and some argue.")

Thus, we recite the blessing, "For making miracles for our fathers" before reading the Megillah on Purim, although the miracles there were disguised as being a part of the natural order.

Each survivor of the German killing fields in Europe had scores of such "personal prepared miracles" in the most critical moments, enabling them to survive.

From the day that the Nazi regime rose to power, a continuous and uninterrupted protective chain of events was extended to many of the survivors. This protection was like a plate of armor shielding from the massive destruction that engulfed countless victims.

It was as if a Heavenly decree prevented harm from coming their way. And so I heard from Rabbi Y. Gustman, that the survival of those who were in Nazi-occupied Europe was the result of a Heavenly decree.

Such Heavenly decrees may be known to some people in advance.[3] As our Sages state, "If one awakens with a Torah verse on his lips, let him see this as a minor prophecy." (Berachos 55b).[4]

---

3 א"ר יוחנן השכים ונפל לו פסוק לתוך פיו הרי זו נבואה קטנה

4 In the story that follows, Rav Grainom records the miracles that saved his

Such dreams may foretell events. "Not interpreting a dream is comparable to not reading a letter." (Berachos 55a).[5]

Although the Sages also teach that "There is no dream without some meaningless content," (Berachos 55a),[6] still, many Sages gave validity to the content of dreams. They understood this statement to mean that by and large, dreams were meaningful.

In his introduction to "Sifra D'Tzniusa," Rav Chaim of Volozhin writes of a man in Vilna who had powers of vision from his dreams. He says that the Gaon of Vilna commented that a "ba'al mareh shechora," a melancholic personality, can have dreams that contain truth—and that is not a reflection of the dreamer's spiritual development.[7]

---

life during World War II. Some of them came about through information he received in his dreams that gave him insight into what was going to unfold in the future. In this introduction, Rav Grainom sets down an understanding of the meaning of miracles and dreams in Torah sources. —EDITOR

5 חלמא דלא מפשר כאגרתא דלא מקריא

6 אי אפשר לחלום בלא דברים בטלים

7 Despite his reluctance to portray himself as worthy of miracles, Rav Grainom notes he feels obligated to share his story because ultimately it is not the level of spiritual development that determines whether a person will be the beneficiary of a miracle. —EDITOR

Thus, I feel obligated to publicize how my personal "hidden" miracles were revealed to me.

Divine intervention, conveyed via dreams, helped me make choices that led to my survival and the survival of others during the Second World War.

2.

FROM YESHIVA, TO THE POLISH ARMY

SUMMER, 1939

DURING THE YEARS 1937–1938 I SERVED IN the Polish army.

I was discharged and returned to yeshiva in September 1938.

In July 1939, six weeks before the outbreak of the war on September 1st, I was re-inducted into the Polish army.

My friends at the yeshiva hid the draft notice until the day I was to depart for induction.

Rav Dovid Blaicher, dean of Beis Yosef in Mezrich, our yeshiva, had been giving me special attention (for reasons unknown to me at the time.) On what was to be my last day at the yeshiva, his hand never left my own. He invited me for a walk and I joined him as he fulfilled his daily communal responsibilities.

Together we visited a sick child. He asked me to bless the child. He told the child's anxious father that because I was a

Kohen he was confident that my blessing would bear fruits. I understood from his exaggerated compliments that he was fortifying my spirit, but I was still puzzled as to the reason.

Rav Dovid's attitude toward army service was unique. All the other yeshivos in Poland gave their army-aged students permission to transfer to yeshivos in what was then Palestine, or had them emigrate and join yeshivos in the independent countries of Latvia and Lithuania.

Rav Dovid felt that this would lead to the Yeshiva's disintegration. Instead, he suggested that the year-and-a-half of required army service amongst gentiles could help produce a physically stronger and more mature student. The experience could enhance his spiritual growth and ability to be of service to his community. Public service, "zichuy harabim," i.e., strengthening individuals and communities religiously, was an integral part of the Beis Yosef-Novardok philosophy. Hence, Rav Dovid saw army service in a different light than others.

Late that final night Rav Dovid invited me to learn some Talmud with him. We continued well past midnight. An older student who usually slept at Rav Dovid's house on a couch left earlier, allowing me to sleep there that night. Generally, I received free lodging from a local homeowner, however, I had to be there by 11 p.m. If my friends and I were up learning late, we slept on the benches in the bais medresh, the study hall.

At dawn I awoke with the words, "Yosef was sold as a servant," on my lips. (Tehillim 105.17).[8]

It was early, so I went back to sleep until the hour of morning prayers. I awoke, and was conscious of a second verse: "Whose foot they afflicted with fetters, his soul was restrained in iron." (Tehillim 105.18).[9] Of course, at the time I had no idea what message, if any, these verses meant to convey.

I was standing next to Rav Dovid after mincha[10] prayers when the draft notice was handed to me. I was to report to Snov near Baronovich. The enlistment order said it was for local border patrol, but we knew that it was part of a larger but low-key national mobilization. Poland was preparing for the German invasion.

I read the notice and exclaimed in astonishment, "This is as I dreamed ... Yosef was sold to be a servant."

---

8 **לְעֶבֶד נִמְכַּר יוֹסֵף**. The sons of Yaakov were towering, righteous men, but due to a personal failing they wrongly suspected their brother Yosef of being a traitor, and sold Yosef into slavery. The Torah describes the trials and tribulations of Yosef in Egypt as a lone Hebrew amongst hostile others.

−EDITOR

9 **עִנּוּ בַכֶּבֶל רגליו בַּרְזֶל בָּאָה נַפְשׁוֹ**

10 Of the three required daily prayers, mincha is the afternoon prayer.

−EDITOR

Rav Dovid was literally shaken and speechless. With effort he murmured, "What are you saying?"

"Nothing, really, except that I dreamed this verse last night," I answered.

[ ]

THREE YEARS EARLIER, IN 1936, I HAD PASSED UP an opportunity to use a visa I was offered to emigrate to America.

I felt no regrets and harbored no resentment against Rav Dovid. It was true that those students who left the country avoided the army experience, but I was confident that my spiritual interests were best served by remaining in the yeshiva.

I remember telling my parents, "America is for businessmen. I wish to remain in yeshiva, to do what I choose to do, to stay here."

As for my second dream: about four and a half years later, while serving in the Russian army, I was dispatched to the front lines to attack the retreating Germans.

My right foot was wounded when I stepped on a small explosive.

Iron particles were embedded in the large toe of my foot.

This, of course, was the realization of the words I had dreamed, "His soul was restrained by iron."

[ ]

THE TRAIN TO SNOV HAD A STOPOVER IN BARONOV-
ich, which was about eighty-five miles to the north. I had two
hours between trains.

I said to myself, "Why, the revered teacher Rav Yisroel Yaakov lives here, and there's a good chance he'll remember me."

Rav Yisroel Yaakov Lubchanski was the Mashgiach[11] at the
yeshiva in Baronovich, and son-in-law of the Alter of Novardok. Perhaps that is why fate had it that I made his acquaintance seven years earlier when I stayed for a week at his yeshiva.

"I'll visit him and ask for his blessing," I thought.

It would be a welcomed help considering the dangerous experience I was about to embark on.

Rav Yisroel Yaakov received me with joy and warmth, as if
he had been waiting for me.

When it was time to leave and continue on to Snov, he gave
me a letter for a certain member of that community. I did not
give the letter much thought and assumed it contained personal business in no way related to me or my situation.

---

11 A senior member of the yeshiva staff responsible for inspiring, uplifting and
challenging the personal growth of the students, often by delivering rousing
talks about personal ethics called "shmuessen."   —EDITOR

Arriving at Snov, I immediately went to the Town Rabbi and gave him a letter of introduction from my yeshiva.

He read it with visible pain and discomfort. With war threatening, the community had lost its ability to provide adequate hospitality.

"How can we arrange for the rabbi[12] to have kosher food in the army camp?"

I felt sympathy for the Rabbi seeing him take my plight so personally.

While he was discussing possible options with his son, I took a second letter out of my pocket and said, "Here, I've brought a letter from Rav Yisroel Yaakov."

"A letter from Rav Yisroel Yaakov! Certainly things will work out," he said with a sigh of relief.

The Rabbi's eyes lit up and he sent his son to deliver the letter.

And things did, with Hashem's help, work out unexpectedly well. The recipient of the letter owned the town mill where grains were ground into flour. He generously supplied me with food and all necessities.

---

12 The young Rav Grainom.   —EDITOR

In addition, to my astonishment, the sergeant in charge of registration and uniform and weapons distribution behaved with good will towards me. He seemed to need me, his "little Jew," to assist with the various administrative details.

[ ]

FURTHERMORE, WE SAW THE HAND OF PROVIDENCE in interesting ways.

At roll call, we were lined up for inspection according to height, the tallest first. The sergeant counted until he reached the last few soldiers in the lineup and dispatched them all to the front line, the border with Germany.

Being quite short, I found myself toward the end of the line. At that point, he declared the quota filled, and the rest of us were told to wait for further transports.

As I became aware of his protective attitude, I, and the other Jewish recruits that I took into confidence, positioned ourselves as close as possible to the rear of all line-ups.

This Divine protection I attributed to the righteous Rav Yisroel Yaakov. The Jewish businessman who owned the local mill had great respect and admiration for him and did all that was humanly possible to help me.

It was due to his strenuous efforts that I was not at the front when the Germans attacked.

They easily massacred the Polish soldiers, who fought against the German tanks . . . with horses.

I said to myself, in the words of Dovid Hamelech, "Behold, the Almighty is my Helper, my Master is with the supporters of my soul." (Tehillim 54.6).[13] "And mankind shall say, 'There is, indeed, reward for the righteous (the Tzadik[14] of Baronovich); there is Hashem who judges in the land." (Tehillim 58.12).[15]

---

13 הִנֵּה אֱלֹקִים עֹזֵר לִי, אֲדֹנָי בְּסֹמְכֵי נַפְשִׁי

14 Righteous man.   —EDITOR

15 וְיֹאמַר אָדָם אַךְ־פְּרִי לַצַּדִּיק, אַךְ יֵשׁ־אֱלֹקִים שֹׁפְטִים בָּאָרֶץ

3.

A PRISONER
OF WAR

OCTOBER–DECEMBER 1939

EARLIER, ON AUGUST 23, 1939, THE GERMANS and Russians signed a Non-Aggression Treaty. On September 1st when the Germans overran Poland from the west, the Russians invaded from the east.

Snov, a district near Baronovich, on the border of Poland, was now occupied by the Russians.

Eighteen Polish officers and soldiers, including myself and one other Jew, were taken as prisoners of war by the Russians. We were marched 45 miles north to Novardok, and locked in a large prison for the night. In the morning, soldiers stationed there marched us eastward toward Russia.

Finally, one evening we arrived at Mir and camped in a large building that was used as a theatre. It was Yom Kippur eve. The streets were empty and through the windows of the Jewish homes I could see the holiday candles.

Afterwards, I was told that a friend and former classmate

whose acquaintance I made at Pinsk yeshiva recognized me as our group entered the town.

That evening, he and a friend bribed the guard to release me. They searched the building but did not find me. I had found a quiet place to pray and sleep on this special holiday, in a small booth. Here, I had some privacy and hoped that the Russians would not find me the next morning.

The yeshiva boys gave up and left, though in the morning the Russians did find me and hastily had me rejoin the group.

When I learned of their failed attempt to rescue me, I wondered why they did not consider that a fellow yeshiva student might seek a hidden, out of the way area to pray on Yom Kippur. Why didn't they call my name?

How different my fate might have been had they succeeded in rescuing me that night. Perhaps I would have learned with them and later follow them when the entire Mirrer Yeshiva went to Kobe, Japan. A short while later they were moved to the Chinese city of Shanghai, which was occupied by the Japanese.[16]

---

[16] Almost the entire Mirrer Yeshiva and a sizable part of the students in most Polish yeshivos relocated to Vilna, Lithuania in early October, 1939. The Mirrer students then embarked on an odyssey that led to their salvation in Shanghai, China for the duration of the war. See *Operation: Torah Rescue* by Yecheskel Leitner, page 22.　　　　　　　　　　　—EDITOR

"The steps of a man are ordered from Hashem, how can a man understand his own way?" (Mishlei 20.24).[17] "The steps of a man are ordered by Hashem and He shall find favor in His way." (Tehillim 37.23).[18]

We reached the city of Kozelsk, and after about six weeks, the Russians sent those that lived in western Poland, now occupied by the Germans, farther into Russia.

Others, like myself, who lived in Eastern Poland—now occupied by the Russians—were released.

I arrived at my parents' home in Lenin, a small town sixty-five miles east of Pinsk.

My younger brother, Avraham Koppel, a student at the Yeshiva in Luniniets, was there. He was trying to find a way to reach Vilna where his yeshiva had joined ranks with the Kletsk yeshiva.

[17] מֵ ה' מִצְעֲדֵי־גָבֶר וְאָדָם מַה־יָּבִין דַּרְכּוֹ

[18] מֵ ה' מִצְעֲדֵי־גֶבֶר כּוֹנָנוּ, וְדַרְכּוֹ יֶחְפָּץ

4.

MY DREAM
OF AKEIDAS
YITZCHOK

JANUARY 1940

IBEGAN LEARNING WITH RAV MOSHE MILSTEIN, our town's rabbi and dayan (judge).

Two weeks after my arrival, I dreamed that I was standing in the synagogue where my father usually stood. My father was the Gabbai[19] and when the Torah was read, he stood at the bimah.[20]

In the dream, my father was called to the Torah and the portion read was Akeidas Yitzchok—our patriarch Avraham heeding Hashem's commandment to bring his son Yitzchok on Mount Moriah as a sacrifice.

---

19 A member of the community appointed or elected to administrate the conducting of public prayer and other communal matters, like charity appeals.
                                                                    —EDITOR

20 A table stationed in the center of the synagogue where the Torah scroll is placed for public reading.   —EDITOR

I could not see any connection between my father and Avraham our patriarch's ordeal.

When I told Rabbi Milstein my dream, he was silent and thoughtful.

After a while, he said, "Maybe it would be best if your brother Avraham Koppel did not go to Vilna. We already know of one yeshiva student from Lenin sent to Siberia by the Russians when they caught him trying to cross the border." He was referring to Moshe Zaychik, now living in Bnai Brak, Israel.

I told my brother and parents of the dream, adding Rabbi Milstein's interpretation.

My brother, who wanted above all to be studying in his yeshiva, considered his situation carefully and decided to take the chance. He made it there successfully.

[ ]

LATER, IN MARCH OF 1940, I, TOO, SNUCK INTO VILNA, bringing him money to pay for a ticket from Kovna to the United States via Russia or Kobe, Japan. From Japan, perhaps he'd get a visa to the United States. A traveler had to prove he could pay for his ticket before applying for a visa.

Years later, in New York, I met one of my brother's friends, Rabbi Chaim Ginsburg. He told me, that at the time, he shared a room with my brother and two other yeshiva students in

Vilna. One day, Russian soldiers came with orders to transport the four of them to Siberia.

My brother, Avraham Koppel, could not bear the thought of being separated from his rabbis and colleagues at the yeshiva. Besides the physical difficulties, living in Siberia meant being jailed in a spiritual desert.

He asked his three friends to hide him beneath their pillows and blankets, choosing to risk his life and remain in Vilna and continue trying to get a visa. His friends went off to Siberia.

In time, Avraham Koppel became another martyr in the long list of rabbis and yeshiva students in Lithuania. And so the content of my dream (about my father being called to the Torah and Akeidas Yitzchok being read) came to be.

If my brother had remained at home in Lenin, or if he had been arrested at the border, or if he had gone to Siberia with his friends, or if he had received an American visa; in any of these instances his chances for survival might have been greater.

He had more than enough money for a ticket, and relatives in New York had given the Vaad Hatzaloh[21] extra money. To

---

21 A communal group organized primarily by Orthodox Jews with the specific goal of raising money and doing everything possible to influence government policy and decision-making to save Jews from certain death in Europe during World War II.   –EDITOR

this day I have in my possession a card from the Vaad Hatzaloh to these relatives informing them that all financial requirements were in order.

[ ]

WHILE IT SEEMS THAT THERE WERE POSSIBILITIES for his survival, practical and reasonable efforts are to no avail if Heaven decreed otherwise.

As the prophet writes in Eicha (3.9), "He had blocked my way with hewn stone, my paths He made crooked."[22]

And in Yeshaya (42.16), "I will lead them in paths that they have not known."[23]

Also Iyov 19.8, "He has fenced up my way, I cannot pass, my paths He has set in darkness."[24]

It is obvious that at the time of my dream, and long before my brother Avraham Koppel perished, as one more Akeidah with all the other millions, the Heavenly decree had already been finalized.

As the verse teaches us, "Hashem had done as He has

---

22 גָּדַר דְּרָכַי בְּגָזִית נְתִיבֹתַי עִוָּה

23 בִּנְתִיבוֹת לֹא־יָדְעוּ אַדְרִיכֵם

24 אָרְחִי גָדַר וְלֹא אֶעֱבוֹר וְעַל נְתִיבוֹתַי חֹשֶׁךְ יָשִׂים

planned, He has fulfilled His word that He had commanded in the days of old." (Eicha 2.17).[25]

Rashi explains that the term "days of old" refers to the time when the Torah was given. At that time, Hashem warned of retribution. (See Vayikra 26.14-46).

Many of our tragedies occur years after the Heavenly decree had ordained them. But always, Hashem's decree truly controls human destiny.

25 עָשָׂה ה׳ אֲשֶׁר זָמָם בִּצַּע אֶמְרָתוֹ אֲשֶׁר צִוָּה מִימֵי־קֶדֶם

5.

HOME IN LENIN, UNDER RUSSIAN OCCUPATION

WINTER, 1940–SPRING, 1941

DURING THE WINTER OF 1940-41, THE NEW border between Russia and Germany was not yet completely closed.

Brisk was a border town. Therefore it was a way-station for many refugees. At that time, people were smuggling themselves into the Russian-held side rather than remain in German-ruled territory.

One day, I left Lenin and travelled ten miles by horse and wagon to Mekahshavitz. There, I boarded the train for a one-hour ride to Luniniets.

At Luniniets, I waited for the westward train to Brisk.

Arriving in Brisk, I snuck across the Bugg river, to German-occupied Slaviticz.

The distance between Lenin and Brisk is about 135 miles.

Three days later, I returned home bringing with me my sister, Sara Gittel, and her two children, Baruch, aged three, and two-year-old Hinda Leah, to live with my parents in Lenin.

Her husband, Rabbi Yaakov Yitzchok Koziollek, remained on the German side in Vlodavah, choosing to stay there with rabbis and teachers of his own yeshiva, formerly in Lubartov. His goal was to reach Vilna, at which time he would send for his wife and children.

Lenin was now under Communist rule. We had all the basic necessities, however, we were all concerned about my brother-in-law and his colleagues. With every passing day that they remained in Vlodavah, the likelihood of their being trapped on the German side of the border increased.

One day, a resident of my town began discussing my sister's situation with me. He seemed genuinely concerned about her having to be separated from her husband.

I told him that the present borders were not permanent, and, in time, she would be reunited with her husband.

I said this quite innocently, hoping that my words might, in themselves, bring about a better reality.

I was unaware that this man was an informer, and that our conversation would be used as sufficient "evidence" to do me harm.

"They shoot in secret at the innocent, suddenly they shoot at him and they are not afraid." (Tehillim 64.5).[26]

A few weeks later, fighting between Russia and Germany broke out, in June 1941.

As the Germans advanced, the Russians prepared to retreat.

I happened to be at home one July afternoon when the Chief Russian Politroock, the head of internal security, paid a visit.

His behavior was casual, as if there were no pressing matters.

After a few minutes of light conversation, he mentioned that his group was retreating but would return in three days.

Instead of making a frivolous comment about his optimism, or even thinking such thoughts in my heart (since to openly laugh could be considered treasonous), I responded sincerely as if I believed that in three days he and his regiment would be back.

"Three days," I repeated in earnest, and added that I hoped the Germans would not manage to slaughter us all during those three days.

The commander seemed to have found satisfactory answers to whatever he was investigating and left.

---

26 לִירֹת בַּמִּסְתָּרִים תָּם, פִּתְאֹם יֹרֻהוּ וְלֹא יִירָאוּ

Obviously, his visit was more than social—he came to check something important.

I could not have known that a miracle had taken place, had I not been told afterwards that someone had squealed on me.

Apparently, the conversation with my fellow townsman regarding the border situation had been interpreted by him, an ardent Communist, as indifference to the plight of the Russians. Or even worse, that I preferred a German occupation, and would be glad to see the Russian Communists forced to retreat.

The purpose of the Politroock's visit was to assess my loyalty.

In general, the N.K.V.D. security forces did not investigate reports of disloyalty, but acted upon them immediately and ruthlessly.

In my case, not only was the information first investigated, but also the investigation was conducted by no less than the senior officer, who then judged me innocent.

"Like the flow of streams of water, so is the king's heart in the hand of Hashem, He turns it wherever He wills." (Mishlei 21.1).[27]

---

27 פַּלְגֵי־מַיִם לֶב־מֶלֶךְ בְּיַד־ ה' ' עַל־כָּל־אֲשֶׁר יַחְפֹּץ יַטֶּנּוּ

[ ]

THE MIDRASH TEACHES THAT BEASTS OF PREY DO not attack a human being unless the person appears to them as another animal, having become debased to animal level. (Midrash Agadah, Noach, 9.2).[28]

These people, with animal spirits, only attack those who wield influence and power and are perceived as threatening.

The security officer considered me a fool for believing the Russians would return in a few days. A simpleton like myself was, in his eyes, no threat to the Communist regime.

From this story of my interrogation by the Russian officer, I realized that Hashem helps not only the wise, to choose their words properly, but also helps the naïve, who do not see the dangers confronting them, and do not know when to keep silent.

A Heavenly decree had protected me.

My replies to his questions were naïve. I accepted his opinion wholeheartedly, and did not express any doubt. Even in my heart, at that critical moment, I did not doubt his words.

וכן אמרו אין חיה הורגת את האדם עד שידמה בעיניה כבהמה. 28

I believe that my facial expression was one of joy and did not show any hesitation in accepting his evaluation of the situation. My reaction was different than it would have been ordinarily, and was perfectly suited to the situation.

"By Dovid, when he changed his behavior before Avimelech,"[29] successfully, "who then drove him away," out of the palace, saving Dovid's life (Tehillim 34.1).[30]

If a person is not wise enough to consciously adapt his behavior to a dangerous situation, Hashem helps him react in the proper behavior mode.

That night, July 17, 1941, the Russians retreated and anyone judged non-supportive of their Communist ideology "disappeared" with them.

Observing the miracle that had taken place, I saw my life in the terms of the psalmist, "I will thank Hashem with my whole

---

29 לְדָוִד בְּשַׁנּוֹתוֹ אֶת־טַעְמוֹ לִפְנֵי אֲבִימֶלֶךְ, When fleeing from King Shaul, who suspected Dovid of trying to usurp the kingdom from him, Dovid attempted to hide in foreign territory. Servants of Achish, king of Gath, recognized Dovid as the famed Jewish general and brought him to the king. Fearing for his life, Dovid changed his demeanor before the king, acting wild and drooling. Achish rebuked his servants for bringing this madman into his house. —EDITOR

30 וַיְגָרְשֵׁהוּ וַיֵּלַךְ

heart, I will sing praises to Your name ... When my enemies
turned back, they stumble ... for You have maintained my right
and my cause ... giving righteous judgment." (Tehillim 9.2-5).[31]

"For You delivered my soul from death, my feet from falling,
that I may walk before Hashem in the light of life." (Tehillim
56.14).[32]

31 : אוֹדֶה ה' בְּכָל־לִבִּי, אֲסַפְּרָה כָּל־נִפְלְאוֹתֶיךָ
אֶשְׂמְחָה וְאֶעֶלְצָה בָךְ, אֲזַמְּרָה שִׁמְךָ עֶלְיוֹן:
בְּשׁוּב־אוֹיְבַי אָחוֹר, יִכָּשְׁלוּ וְיֹאבְדוּ מִפָּנֶיךָ:
כִּי־עָשִׂיתָ מִשְׁפָּטִי וְדִינִי, יָשַׁבְתָּ לְכִסֵּא
שׁוֹפֵט צֶדֶק:

32 כִּי הִצַּלְתָּ נַפְשִׁי מִמָּוֶת הֲלֹא רַגְלַי מִדֶּחִי,
לְהִתְהַלֵּךְ לִפְנֵי אֱלֹקִים בְּאוֹר הַחַיִּים

6.

LENIN UNDER GERMAN OCCUPATION

SUMMER, 1941—SPRING, 1942

THE RUSSIANS WERE GONE, AND WE WERE NOW under German occupation.

By September, 1941, approximately two months after the Germans' arrival, they were preparing to kill all the Jews in our area.

Without much public awareness, efforts were made to distract and dissuade the Nazis from their plans.

A miracle took place, and although an SS unit remained stationed on the outskirts of our town, miraculously, no one was killed.

I realized the extent of the miracle, when, one day, our town Rabbi, Moshe Milstein, told me that a friendly and helpful gentile woman told his wife that there was not one Jew left alive in the neighboring city of Pinsk.

Upon hearing this tragic news, I felt that Rav Milstein and the Jews of my town had few options.

Where could someone such as Rav Milstein, with his wife and five small children, go?

To discuss the situation publicly would create chaos. Some people might escape into the forests to hide, but this would endanger those left behind.

Like a deaf mute, I said nothing.

Maybe the gentiles were spreading rumors to create panic?

Could it be... the entire Jewish population of Pinsk–killed?

[ ]

ONE MORNING, THE RABBI RELATED TO ME A DREAM he had dreamt that disturbed him.

In his dream, he found himself in the home of an old friend. The house was flooded with great amounts of light. When he looked to the side, he saw through an open door that, in another room, the light was even brighter!

"Who is there?" he called out.

The Mashgiach's name, Rav Yerucham Levovitz, of the Mirrer Yeshiva, was answered.

I listened to his dream without commenting. I understood that Rav Milstein could interpret the dream for himself. In a short time, he would find himself in the next world, and be in the company of Rav Levovitz, who had passed away a few years before.

Rav Milstein, a great and holy man, suffered greatly.

Once, when I arrived for our learning session, I saw, to my surprise, that the rabbi no longer had a beard.

Two Germans, who were not part of the official occupation force, had a habit of harassing local Jews for "pleasure."

When an argument broke out between a Jewish and a gentile woman, the two Germans came immediately to the scene. They took the two young children of the Jewish woman out into the courtyard, and set their vicious dog on them. Both children were brutally killed.

These cruel beasts had cut off his beard.

Another time, late at night, one of the two came with a local gentile and ordered us all out of our beds.

They drew their guns and demanded that we lie on the floor–and sing.

Frozen with fear, no one made a sound.

I was worried that our silence would infuriate them, so I began to say in a loud voice, "Recite hymns to Him, sing to Him, tell of His wondrous works." (Tehillim 105.2).[33]

In this passage, the name of Hashem is not mentioned

---

33 שִׁירוּ־לוֹ זַמְּרוּ־לוֹ, שִׂיחוּ בְּכָל־נִפְלְאוֹתָיו

openly. It was appropriate to recite it, since we had not washed our hands,[34] nor were we fully dressed.

In retrospect, this is how I understood my choice of words, though, at the time, shaking with the fear of imminent death, I chose the words instinctively without forethought.

Not long after this, one of the two Germans again came into our house, and called me into another room.

He stood me against the wall, and, with his finger on the trigger of his gun, said, "Tell me, who in town has guns or ammunition?"

Again, almost unconsciously, and without effort or thought, I answered, calmly, and with confidence, "A while back the local government ordered all citizens to hand over guns and ammunition to the police, and we all did so."

The Nazi seemed satisfied with the answer, and left.

"The plans of the heart belong to man, but from Hashem are the utterances of the tongue." (Mishlei 16.1).[35]

---

34   In order to accord proper honor to Torah and the name of G-d, Jewish law requires that upon awakening, one should have his or her body covered with a certain minimum of garments, and to wash each hand alternately (right, then left) three times, to remove spiritual contamination, before saying blessings or saying the name of G-d.   —EDITOR

35   לְאָדָם מַעַרְכֵי־לֵב וּמֵ ה' מַעֲנֵה לָשׁוֹן

At a time when a person is unable to organize his thoughts, Heaven will supply appropriate words.

[ ]

THERE WERE OTHER INSTANCES WHERE THESE TWO Nazis caused great misery to our community.

People preferred not to retell the humiliating incidents, and instead, focused themselves on the continuing effort of survival.

However, Divine justice eventually caught up with these two beasts.

One day, when I was walking past the Wehrmacht,[36] I saw one of the two Nazis hanging from a pole. The pole was not too high, and his feet were barely off the ground, but I could tell he was dead.

A great fright overcame me when I saw a policeman in a doorway, peeking out and observing passers-by.

Assuming he was studying our reactions, I immediately lowered my head, so that I could not see the body or have the policeman see the expression on my face.

---

36 The Germans called their army, leading up to and through World War II, 'the Wehrmacht.' Rav Grainom refers here to an army base stationed in his village from which the Germans governed. —EDITOR

Because every moment was filled with danger, and the knowledge that the lives of our loved ones were constantly under threat, there was really not much to celebrate.

Still, "when the wicked perish, there is joy." (Mishlei 11.10).[37]

It was good to see the mortality of this sadist who had been oppressing us, and it allowed for hope that, in time, revenge and justice would prevail.

"For it is the day of Hashem's vengeance, and the year of recompense, for the cause of Tzion." (Yeshaya 34.8).[38]

"But You, Almighty One, will bring them down into the pit of destruction, bloody and deceitful men shall not live out half their lives, but I shall trust in You." (Tehillim 55.24).[39]

The story behind the death of the German soldier surfaced, in due time.

They were paratroopers who were dropped behind Russian front lines, on a special mission.

Instead of returning to their unit, they took their "fun and adventure" against the Jewish population.

---

37 וּבַאֲבֹד רְשָׁעִים רִנָּה

38 כִּי יוֹם נָקָם לַ ה' שְׁנַת שִׁלּוּמִים לְרִיב צִיּוֹן

39 וְאַתָּה אֱלֹקִים תּוֹרִדֵם לִבְאֵר שַׁחַת אַנְשֵׁי דָמִים וּמִרְמָה לֹא־יֶחֱצוּ יְמֵיהֶם, וַאֲנִי אֶבְטַח־בָּךְ

Then they made a mistake.

They angered the gentile farmers, by subjecting them to cruel pranks and the like.

The German Wehrmacht commander did not want civil unrest.

He had the two deserters court-martialed, and executed publicly, by hanging, to pacify the local population.

7.

IN THE
HANZOVITCH
LABOR CAMP

SPRING–SUMMER, 1942

FOR THE TWO-AND-A-QUARTER YEARS SINCE being sent home by the Russians, I learned with Rav Milstein.

On the day after Pesach, 1942, I told him that I would not return for our afternoon session.

"Why?" he asked.

I explained, "As you know, sixty of us are being sent to the Hanzovitch labor camp and I am one of them."

"It can't be," said the rabbi. "The Jewish Council promised not to include you, after I told them that our town has only one ben Torah . . . I asked that you be exempted."

The Jewish Council, composed of respectable members of the community, who heeded their rabbi, found 59 able-bodied bachelors. A possible sixtieth, a refugee from Warsaw, was recovering from typhus and the Jewish doctor had excused him from any work for two weeks.

How could I let them send a married man in my place?

I had no choice but to go, unless a volunteer could be found to replace me.

As I was preparing to depart, my father came to me and said that he would go in my place.

I answered him, "Do we know with any certainty that it is safer to remain here than it is to join the work group? Since fate has called me to the labor camp, I will go."

[ ]

AFTER SHAVUOUS, ALL ABLE-BODIED MEN FROM OUR town, including my older brother Moshe, were ordered to be sent to Hanzovitch to join our work group. Married, with a five-year-old son, he had not been included in the first group.

However, before Shavuos arrived, the fellow from Warsaw recovered from his bout with typhus.

He felt his chances for survival were greater with his friends from the first work group—because the first group was all young and unmarried, and thus, more suited to escaping and surviving in the forests.

He went to the Jewish Council and volunteered to take my place in the labor camp.[40]

---

40 Apparently, the first group of bachelors remained a distinct group. Even though all able-bodied men were being called up to the labor camp at this later

The Jewish Council was pleased by this development. Here was an opportunity to fulfill the rabbi's request, that I be allowed to continue to study with him. They went to the police and explained that a volunteer had been found to take my place in Hanzovitch.

It is important to remind the reader that the general atmosphere was calm, and life continued with relative regularity. By now, we had been under German occupation for almost two years.

No one imagined that the Germans were planning to kill all the Jews in Europe. The Final Solution was an undreamed nightmare. For this reason, people were willing to volunteer for labor camps and work details.

The now-healthy refugee from Warsaw arrived in Hanzovitch to take my place.

That day, at work, a gentile whispered to a member of our group that the Germans had prepared a grave for one of us.

How did he know? Each day the Germans executed one or two prisoners. It was usually Russian soldiers who had been captured earlier, during the German invasion.

The gentile explained that, since no Russian had been executed that day, it appeared that the grave was meant for one of us.

---

date, after Shavuos, the Warsaw bachelor who recovered from typhus specifically requested to be assigned to fill Rav Grainom's place.   —EDITOR

The bloodthirsty Nazis needed their sacrifice every day.

Later that day, a Nazi came to our camp asking for, "Lese-bik, who is not fit for work."

The head of our group, a Jewish refugee from Lodz, Poland, was away in Lenin getting supplies.

His assistant stepped forward and answered wisely, "I am the assistant temporarily in charge, and I do not know any Jew with that name."

He went over the list as if to double-check. No, there was no Lesebik. Of course, he knew who they meant.

He then assured the Nazi that all those on the list were healthy and productive workers, none having any limitations whatsoever.

Until then, I had been assigned kitchen duty. The people from my home town dealt with me kindly and assigned me to this lighter, less physical work. I was happy with this arrangement because being the chef's assistant meant I did not have to transgress the Shabbos, at least not with melocha d'Oraisa, Biblically forbidden activities.[41]

---

[41] The framework of Jewish law consists of the 613 mitzvos recorded in the Torah given to Moshe, which encompasses the entire spectrum of Jewish life on the individual, social and national level. Because some confusion may arise over points of the Biblical law where forbidden activities may be similar to permitted ones, the early Sages of the generation of Ezra promulgated a body

After this close call, the head of the work force suggested that I join the main group that went into the forests to cut down trees to be used in improving the roads.

If any more questions were asked regarding my ability to work, he could answer, "He is one of the best workers–able to do the most difficult tasks."

I agreed and prayed, "See my affliction and pain, and forgive all my sins." (Tehillim 25.18).[42]

Forgive even the sin of jeopardizing our lives, "like one who grabs a dog by the ears." (Mishlei 26.17).[43] So did we bring the Nazi beast on ourselves.

We had been naïve to let the Germans know I was unsuited for work.

---

of decrees intended to make the law more consistent and easy to remember. (See Derech Chaim to Avos 1.1). These rabbinic enactments are known in Jewish law as enactments "d'Rabbonon" which are built atop the framework of the original mitzvos of the Torah, which are known by the Aramaic term "d'Oraisa." In practice, a Jew is required to uphold all the enactments d'Rabbonon as well as the mitzvos d'Oraisa, but if one would be forced due to life-threatening circumstances, it is better to violate a d'Rabbonon enactment than to perform an act prohibited d'Oraisa. —EDITOR

42 רְאֵה עָנְיִי וַעֲמָלִי, וְשָׂא לְכָל־חַטֹּאותָי

43 מַחֲזִיק בְּאָזְנֵי־כָלֶב עֹבֵר מִתְעַבֵּר עַל־רִיב לֹא־לוֹ

"My eyes are ever toward Hashem, He will free my trapped feet." (Tehillim 25.15).[44]

May we merit, "you will tread on the lion and viper," and still not be hurt. (Tehillim 91.13).[45]

With Hashem's kindness this episode ended well. The Germans did not ask about me again.

---

44 עֵינַי תָּמִיד אֶל־ ה' , כִּי הוּא־יוֹצִיא מֵרֶשֶׁת רַגְלָי

45 תִּרְמֹס כְּפִיר וְתַנִּין

8.
THE ESCAPE

AUGUST 1942

ONE DAY MY BROTHER MOSHE TOLD ME THAT Yerachmiel Dvorin, a neighbor from Lenin, invited us to be included in his small group when, and if, an escape by all the labor camp inmates was attempted.

We all feared that the Germans would carry out their threat: if one person escaped, ten laborers and twenty relatives at home would be killed in retribution.

In fact, we suspected that the Germans might be even more barbaric than that, since a successful escape would point to collaboration with Russian partisans. We feared they might kill all our loved ones at home who were now crowded together in the recently-formed ghetto.

Fearing this possibility, plans for escape were formulated, but not acted upon, temporarily held in abeyance.

A word of praise and admiration is due the refugees from Warsaw. They were bachelors without families to protect. They could have been concerned only with their own survival. Yet, out of deference to us, they did not attempt to escape, and thereby endanger us and our families.

Logic and common sense dictated that Moshe and I should join Yerachmiel Dvorin, should an escape be attempted.

He was sharp, capable, and had much life experience.

Through his business endeavors, he had become quite familiar with the surrounding countryside.

He was respected and appreciated by the farmers and peasants because he brought business to the area. In the winter months, when the swamps were frozen over, they would cut down trees and transport them by sled to dry land. In the summer, the trees were burned in a way that produced tar.

Without this income, the peasants would have been poverty-stricken.

I was considering his invitation and was inclined to accept it. However, a few nights before, I had a dream which gave me second thoughts.[46]

---

46   From what Rav Grainom indicates later, he had this dream before Dvorin approached his brother Moshe with the invitation to join his escape group.

—EDITOR

He was the ideal comrade-in-arms, and I would have joyously thanked Hashem for this capable partner, considering the dangers inherent in wandering the forest and countryside.

But remembering my dream and how I had interpreted it in my sleep, I told my brother with finality that I was not interested in joining Yerachmiel's escape group, but that he should feel free to decide for himself.

I knew that with my refusal, I was placing my brother in a most uncomfortable dilemma. Moshe, without being able to explain why, decided not to separate from me, should an escape be attempted. Perhaps out of protective brotherly love, he could not leave me, his younger brother, to go off with our neighbor's group.

Perhaps he believed that Divine Providence would sooner protect a yeshiva student than one not engaged in spiritual pursuits. I was totally unsuited to survive forests teeming with dangers. Russian partisans unsympathetic to Jews, especially religious Jews, roamed, searching for prey.

I was quite happy with his decision. I felt certain that it would bode us both well.

A while before having this dream, my brother made contact with a gentile who lived nearby. He was willing to help us hide, and not turn us into the Nazis, should we escape.

[ ]

ON FRIDAY AFTERNOON, THE SECOND DAY OF ROSH Chodesh Elul 1942 (August 14, 1942), a Nazi brought his car for servicing to the garage where a member of our group worked.

"Clean it well," he ordered.

"From where have you come?" the prisoner asked.

"From Lenin."

"And how are things in Lenin?" he asked.

The Nazi answered, "Lenin is kaput."

He described in detail the killing that began at two in the morning and continued all night. He boasted that the efficiency and organization resulted in a "Judenrein" Lenin, not one Jew left alive.

The news quickly spread throughout the labor camp, however, I heard nothing at my workstation.

When I entered the barracks, I noticed preparations being finalized for the escape.

My brother hastened me to eat what little bread was available. Since it was Friday, I preferred to daven[47] first, and let the

---

64

eating wait for darkness, at which point, I could recite kiddush over the bread.[48]

Besides the terrible news regarding Lenin, word reached the camp that partisans had attacked the nearby city of Fahaust. More than half the inmates were from there, and they insisted that the escape begin, so that they could return to Fahaust and protect their families from the German savagery.

As I was placing my tefillin[49] in my pocket, the breakout began. Exiting in haste from the windows and doors, three hundred and fifty prisoners ran off in the direction of the forest.

My brother directed me to an abandoned shack in the nearby courtyard. Here, we were to wait for the gentile to come and give us shelter, as he had promised.

---

48 The Torah commands the Jewish people, "Remember the Shabbos day, to sanctify it." The Sages enacted that this mitzvah of verbal declaration, called "kiddush," should be fulfilled by reciting a blessing to the Almighty over a cup of wine at the commencement of Shabbos Friday night. In the event that wine is not available, the blessing of "kiddush" can be made over bread. —EDITOR

49 The Torah commands a Jewish man to place tefillin, specially made black boxes containing parchments inscribed with selected Biblical passages, on his head (shel rosh) and on his arm (shel yad), bound in place by black leather straps. A Jewish man is required to wear tefillin during the morning prayer service.
—EDITOR

Upon entering the shack, I instinctively felt that it was dangerous to remain there. The shack did not seem a good place to hide, and besides, I was not willing to put my life in the trust of a gentile.

Without a moment's hesitation, I pushed a wooden board from its place,[50] said to Moshe, "Let's go," and we slipped out.

Like the others, we ran in the direction of the forests.[51]

Most of us survived this episode, though my neighbor, Yerachmiel Dvorin and his small group, did not.

They hid themselves nearby, waiting for the cover of darkness, before continuing to the forests.[52] The Germans found them, and hung them in the town center.

---

[50] Rav Grainom likely felt it was dangerous to exit the shack from the front door and found a less conspicuous way for him and his brother to exit. –EDITOR

[51] As an interesting side note, Rav Grainom reports that the German soldier's bragging about the destruction of Lenin, and the subsequent breakout, took place on a Friday afternoon. By Friday night, he and his brother had escaped to the forest. His prophetic dream was set in the forest, on a Friday night.

–EDITOR

[52] In an interview, Rav Grainom told a reporter that since Dvorin knew a lot of peasants in the area from his business dealings, Dvorin was sure that they would protect and guide him to safety. "Living History: A Memorable Visit with Rav Grainom Lazewnik," by Rabbi Eliezer Brand, *Ami Magazine*, Issue 513, April 16, 2021 (21 Iyar 5781), p. 127. As Rav Grainom wrote earlier in this book, he refused to rely on the promises made to his brother by a non-Jewish villager. –EDITOR

[ ]

LIKE THE EARLIER DREAM WHERE MY FATHER WAS
called to the Torah portion of Akeidas Yitzchok, the dream I
will relate now also was realized, though this time, the interpretation saved our life.

In the dream, I found myself in the forest on a Friday evening.

A Jewish family was about to begin their Shabbos meal, and
they invited me to be their guest.

The table was set with fresh Shabbos challah. I wondered to
myself how they managed to arrange this in the middle of a war.

During the dream, I thought to myself, "It's for the best that
my neighbor, Mr. Yerachmiel Dvorin is not here with me.
Dvorin's personality would clash with this family gathering,
and I would be unable to accept their invitation."

At the time, I had no explanation for Dvorin's appearance
in my dream.

Although we were in the same work camp, I had little contact with him.

This dream occurred a few days before he suggested to my
brother that we join him, in the event of an escape attempt.

Dvorin was a successful and learned man, and was admired
by the town folk. My impression of him was from a conversa-

tion he had with my father on a long winter night over a glass of tea when I was five or six years old.

I interpreted the dream to mean that our fates were in no way linked.

[ ]

THE TALMUD SAYS THAT, "A DREAM THAT IS INTER-preted within the dream" [53] is one type of "dreams that are destined to be fulfilled." (Berachos 55b).[54]

Thus, I decided not to accept our neighbor's invitation, thereby saving Moshe and myself from a bitter and humiliating death.

Yerachmiel Dvorin had possessed a noble and good-natured

---

[53] As Rav Grainom explained above, during the dream he "interpreted" the events around him, saying that he was glad that Dvorin was not with him, as his personality would clash with the family gathering. This seemingly irrele-vant thought of Dvorin in the dream, Rav Grainom tells us here, he considered "an interpretation of the dream within the dream." Later, when Rav Grainom concluded that their fates were in no way linked, he felt certain that this was destined to come to pass.   —EDITOR

[54] ואמר ר' יוחנן ג' חלומות מתקיימין
חלום שנפתר בתוך חלום

character.

The tragedy of his execution brought to mind the Talmudic teaching, "Love your neighbor as yourself... choose a bearable death for him." (Sanhedrin 45a).[55] I now understood how much a condemned man is concerned with the way he is killed, once he has resigned himself to a death sentence.

Although my life remained in danger, when I heard of the tragic and humiliating execution of Dvorin and his group, I was more grateful to Hashem for sparing me from such a dreadful type of death, than for still being alive.

The humiliating execution of our neighbors, Dvorin and the Galenson brothers, which stood in contrast to their courageous deeds in trying to save their neighbors, caused me great anguish, and many words of the prophets flashed through my mind.

"How long, Hashem, will you be angry forever, will Your jealousy burn like fire?" (Tehillim 79.5).[56]

"The noble of Yisroel is slain upon high places (publicly),

---

55 אמר רבה בר אבוה אמר קרא ואהבת
לרעך כמוך ברור לו מיתה יפה

56 עַד־מָה ה' תֶּאֱנַף לָנֶצַח,
תִּבְעַר כְּמוֹ־אֵשׁ קִנְאָתֶךָ

how the mighty have fallen." (Shmuel 2, 1.19).[57]

"I am distressed for you, my brother." (Shmuel 2, 1.26).[58]

I prayed, "We became an object of disgrace to our neighbors, a scorn and derision to those around us ... and repay our neighbors (invading enemies) sevenfold into their bosom–their insult that they have disgraced You." (Tehillim 79.4, 79.12).[59]

---

57 הַצְּבִי יִשְׂרָאֵל עַל־בָּמוֹתֶיךָ חָלָל אֵיךְ נָפְלוּ גִבּוֹרִים

58 צַר־לִי עָלֶיךָ אָחִי

59 הָיִינוּ חֶרְפָּה לִשְׁכֵנֵינוּ, לַעַג וָקֶלֶס לִסְבִיבוֹתֵינוּ
וְהָשֵׁב לִשְׁכֵנֵינוּ שִׁבְעָתַיִם אֶל־חֵיקָם, חֶרְפָּתָם אֲשֶׁר
חֵרְפוּךָ אֲדֹנָי

9.

THE ANGEL
GAVRIEL SAVES
OUR LIVES

FALL, 1942

WITH THE LIGHT OF THE NEXT MORNING, WE became aware that we were a group of about fifty. Surrounding us on all sides were dense forests.

We divided ourselves into smaller groups to increase the chances of being accepted by the partisan fighters. At first, I was part of a group of eighteen. Then we separated into groups of nine, until later, when I joined the engineer Mordechai Zaychik and his companion, Nachum Paraphluchick. Nachum was young, and clung to Mordechai Zaychik for protection and security.

That night, the four of us were off.

Navigating with the aid of the stars, we headed northeast, leaving Poland, and entered what had been Russia before the war.

Here, we felt less threatened. The local citizens did not actively persecute Jews, nor did they willingly collaborate with the Germans. The cities were controlled by the Germans, but in the villages and forests, the partisans dominated.

Everyone was suspicious and fearful of each other, but to persecute any group, including Jews, without reason was unacceptable. The Germans were the common enemy.

In these parts, we moved about by day. We met a few groups of partisans, but they were not willing to have us.

Some were anti-Semitic, and cloaked their rejection in strategic rhetoric: "Your community is not composed of good fighters."

Others were more practical and explained that they had enough fighters, but lacked weapons, asking, "Why do you come with empty hands?"

Some partisan leaders were more condescending and said, "You gave your jewelry and gold watches to the Germans. How can you come to us, now, for protection?"

Meanwhile, we heard that two friends from our original group were killed by the partisans, who claimed to have found German documents on them. Then, the partisans spread rumors that the Germans sent Jews into the forests as spies. Jews, the partisans claimed, were willing to spy and therefore save themselves.

The "documents" in question were standard identity cards, that Jews had to carry at all times.

The partisans refused to consider the explanation.

"How could you surrender your Soviet passports to the enemy, in exchange for their identity card?" they asked.

One day, while wandering on side roads, hoping to at last find a sympathetic ear, a partisan with officer's rank approached us.

Riding on a horse, with an automatic rifle slung across his chest, he quickly dismounted and began to shout in a murderous voice, "Run at once into the forest! Go!"[60]

Mordechai and Nachum ran immediately to the forest.

My brother Moshe also took a few steps in retreat, but when he saw that I remained in place, he stopped and shouted at me, "Quick, run!"

I had noticed the partisan's knees were trembling. I sensed that his trembling was due to a fit of inner rage—he was going to shoot us.

If I were to turn my back, he could later claim that he came across spies in the forest, who did not heed his order to halt. Perhaps he would receive recognition, or even a medal for his

---

60 Elsewhere, Rav Grainom told the story to a reporter in this way: "One day, our little group was walking along the side of the road when a high-ranking partisan pulled up, got off his horse, unslung the automatic rifle from his chest, and yelled, "Run into the forest!" "Living History," *Ami Magazine*, Issue 513, April 16, 2021 (21 Iyar 5781), pg. 127.   –EDITOR

alertness. Or maybe he would get a perverse pleasure from murdering us?

My heart dictated that I not turn my back to him, though he continued to order me, "Into the forest!"

His finger was on the trigger.

"Gavriel, Gavriel," I said quietly to myself, summoning the angel Gavriel seven times.

His knees stopped shaking and he lowered his gun.

"What are you mumbling?" he asked.

"I'm saying that we have no possessions," I said, and I lifted my hands as if to say, "Here, check my pockets."

Moshe quickly came forward and continued. "We did not give our valuables to the Germans, we buried them. Give us a chance to avenge the blood of our loved ones. My wife, my son, my mother and father and sister have all been killed. We will attack Lenin and any valuables recovered will be yours. We are only interested in revenge."

The partisan mounted his horse and ordered, "Get out of here, and make sure I never see any of you again."

And he rode off.

10.

WHY I CHOSE SILENCE

WE CONTINUED WALKING IN ABSOLUTE silence. We all felt the close brush with death.

It was imperative that we leave this area, but we didn't know which direction to take.

Feeling overwhelmed by the "open" and clearly observable miracle, I was unable to tell my companions about the "segulah" [61] I had invoked.

I felt it improper to share the above story because I did not want to give the impression that I or our small group had special merits which made us more deserving of being saved than anyone else. This was an instance where my heart understood, yet I felt my capacity for verbal expression was limited.

---

61 An action that is believed to be packed with a spiritual or mystical power to bring about a desired result.   –EDITOR

I had learned about this "segulah" in my youth, from my dear friend Rabbi Leib Weisner. We were together on a summer vacation in a town near Pinsk. In the shul, he found a book which discussed many types of segulos.

All I could remember from that book then, as now, is the one particular segulah which came miraculously to my mind at that most critical moment.[62]

We continued walking in absolute silence. At that time, I could not explain why an "open miracle" had happened to us, and not to so many others that perished?

Today, in retrospect, I find it quite simple. Just as those holy martyrs could not undo the negative decree against them, so too, the murderous ones could not kill anyone whom Heaven had decreed to survive.

After this incident, I whispered to myself, "He will order His angels to guard you on all your paths." (Tehillim 91.11).[63]

As the road stretched on long before us, and no one knew what dangers might confront us tomorrow, I prayed, "Until now, Your tender mercies have helped us, Your loving kindness

---

62   To say the name of the angel Gavriel seven times, when encountering a murderer. Explained by Rav Grainom in *Ami Magazine*, Issue 513, pg 127.

—EDITOR

63   כִּי מַלְאָכָיו יְצַוֶּה־לָּךְ, לִשְׁמָרְךָ בְּכָל־דְּרָכֶיךָ

has not left us, do not forsake us Hashem forever." (Shabbos prayer, "Nishmas").[64]

Come what may, I thanked Hashem for my ability to recognize His kindness to us in these dark times.

"Blessed be the Almighty, Who has not turned away my prayer, nor His steadfast love from me." (Tehillim 66.20).[65] "Lo-heissir," Hashem did not remove the potential for prayer from myself.

Furthermore, "Lo-heissir chassdo," He did not remove His kindness.

By praying, we declare our belief that all is in the hands of Heaven.

Thereby, we become deserving of Hashem's kindness. To an appreciative recipient, Hashem continues to bestow kindness.

These were my thoughts, but as I said, I did not share them with the others. "Since the heart gave no words to express, to whom will the mouth reveal?" (Midrash, Tehillim 9.2).[66] In those difficult moments, silence seemed to be most appropriate.

---

64 עַד הֵנָּה עֲזָרוּנוּ רַחֲמֶיךָ. וְלֹא עֲזָבוּנוּ חֲסָדֶיךָ. וְאַל תִּטְּשֵׁנוּ יְיָ אֱלֹקֵינוּ לָנֶצַח

65 בָּרוּךְ אֱלֹקִים אֲשֶׁר לֹא־הֵסִיר תְּפִלָּתִי וְחַסְדּוֹ מֵאִתִּי

66 ליבא לפומא לא גלי פומא למאן גלי

[ ]

I RECENTLY HAD OPPORTUNITY TO SEE THIS MIRA-
cle recorded. Mordechai Zaychik's book, "From the Diary of a
Partisan/Holocaust Survivor" (Tel Aviv, 1971). On page 84,
he writes:

"At the moment, a miracle took place. The partisan officer's
finger was on the trigger, about to shoot us, when suddenly it
slackened, and he moved his rifle to the side. Grainom Lazewnik, the younger of two brothers, was G-d fearing and studied
in our yeshiva before the war with the goal of being a rabbi or
teacher. During the ordeal, he managed in a most remarkable
way to maintain his composure. Who can say what fate awaited
us, had not Moshe Lazewnik then come forward to eloquently
explain, argue, and plead our case."

This was Mordechai's observation, and from his standpoint,
it was correct.

He did not know of the extraordinary power that had weak-
ened the partisan's will, and had calmed him enough for my
brother to be inspired to approach with his entreaty.

He did not hear my whispering, and I only regret that I
never told him about it. (So how could he know the truth.)

11.

JOINING THE
PARTISANS

NOVEMBER 1942

WE CONTINUED OUR WANDERINGS, AND HAD various adventures, as the High Holiday season, and then Sukkos, passed.

The nights became colder, and we wandered alone in the vast forest and swampy countryside.

"Even a sparrow finds a house and the swallow a nest for herself." (Tehillim 84.4).[67]

"I lift up my eyes to the mountains. From where shall my help come?" (Tehillim 121.1).[68]

Even as long, dark nights end, so, too, we at last arrived at a partisan base.

Until then, we had met small bands of partisans, but now

---

[67] גַּם־צִפּוֹר מָצְאָה בַיִת וּדְרוֹר קֵן לָהּ

[68] אֶשָּׂא עֵינַי אֶל־הֶהָרִים מֵאַיִן יָבֹא עֶזְרִי

we found ourselves at the entrance to a major base. Just being there, was in itself dangerous, because we could be accused of spying: how did we know about this place, and such.

However, as the verse says, "You shall stretch forward your hand against the wrath of my enemies, Your right hand will save me." (Tehillim 138.7).[69]

And so it was.

The sun was setting as we arrived at that front gate. Besides the one, lone guard standing there, was no less than the commander of the base. He was scanning the horizon, as if waiting for us.

At first, he gave us standard answers. "We already have a few Jews who help us with various administrative tasks. Just recently, we accepted two more, a father and a son who are tailors. Of what use are any of you? I have no more room." He insinuated that partisans do not accept anyone for the sole purpose of giving them shelter.

This time, my brother Moshe was truly inspired and boldly said, "I am an expert photographer. I will photograph your military operations. You will have permanent documentation for future generations."

What might seem a ridiculous extravagance to partisans

---

69 עַל אַף אֹיְבַי תִּשְׁלַח יָדֶךָ, וְתוֹשִׁיעֵנִי יְמִינֶךָ

warring against an adversary as great as the German army, actually found favor in his eyes. (Though not as Moshe had suggested. He sent Moshe to serve in the headquarters of the partisans, where his talents could be put to use.)

In the course of this conversation, Moshe repeatedly mentioned that I was his brother, and pleaded that I also be allowed to join. The commander absolutely refused.

I recalled the verse, "My Master, open my lips, that my mouth will praise You." (Tehillim 51.17).[70]

"Open my lips," now, "And my mouth will praise You," always. I will always remember to tell of Your praise.

With confidence that Hashem would accept my heartfelt prayer, I began to plead my case.

"I served in the Polish army, and I can fight the enemy as well as anyone else. I will join the saboteurs . . ."

The commander looked at me with amazement and derision. He probably said to himself, "The nerve of this ragged, short and scrawny-looking Jew."

He ordered me to follow him into the courtyard where a small, one-room house stood. Inside, on a table, were a number of German rifles.

---

70 אֲדֹנָי שְׂפָתַי תִּפְתָּח, וּפִי יַגִּיד תְּהִלָּתֶךָ

"Do you know how to use this?" he asked, handing me one of the weapons.

I opened the rifle, and checked the chamber, making sure it was empty. I closed the gun, aimed at an imaginary target in the distance, and pulled the trigger.

"If you sight a German at three hundred meters (1,000 feet), what would you do?" he asked.

"At that distance, the bullet would rise about fifteen centimeters (six inches) above the target. To compensate, I would aim at his waist in order to hit his heart."

I passed his test! We rejoined the others, and the commander said to Mordechai and Nachum, "I will accept these two. You two, climb the hill over there in the distance, and go to the house that is just visible from here. Tell Ivanov that I took two of you, and he should also take two."

It would have been naïve to accept the commander's suggestion without protest. Could we be sure that the commander was telling the truth about his friend on the hilltop?

Mordechai began to plead with the commander. "We have been travelling together as a group, please do not separate us now."

The commander would not be budged. "Do as I say," he ordered and walked off.

I turned to Mordechai and the silent Nachum and said, "At present, the commander is unapproachable. Do as he says. If Ivanov does not accept you, return in the morning, and we will try with the commander again."

12.

IN RETROSPECT: SELF-DOUBT

A FEW YEARS AFTER THE WAR ENDED, ENGINEER Mordechai Zaychik unburdened his heart to a mutual friend, of his disappointment with my behavior that day.

"From a yeshiva student, I would have expected more loyalty and comradeship," he said.

Mordechai was our leader since the escape, a seven-week ordeal of wandering in the forests. He would speak for us when we met up with partisans, and our travel plans were made according to his judgment.

Mordechai felt I should have categorically said to the commander that I would not separate from my comrades. If the commander would not have all four of us, I should have stayed with Mordechai and the younger Nachum until the situation was settled to the satisfaction of everyone involved.

Mordechai reminded our mutual friend that a while before the incident above took place, we were taking a mid-day rest when Nachum fell asleep. Mordechai suggested that the three of us continue on, and leave Nachum to fend for himself.

We were on the outskirts of a village, and Nachum could manage on his own. Mordechai knew that as a group of three, our chances for acceptance into the partisans was greater.

Although I agreed in principle that there was no immediate danger to Nachum if he were to remain alone in the village, I refused to go along with this idea. By this time, Nachum clung to Mordechai like a child to his mother, and I feared that in his miserable and depressed state, he would suffer great loneliness, and perhaps panic.

Now, Mordechai saw himself burdened by Nachum's presence, because when my brother and I were accepted into the partisans, if not for Nachum, Mordechai, being the only one remaining, would not have been rejected and sent off. Mordechai relates in his book (page 90) that, later on, he refused an opportunity to join a group of partisans, because they were not willing to include Nachum.

According to the teaching of Ben Piturah, "Let them both drink and both die, and not any one of them see his friend die,"

(Bava Metzia 62a),[71] it would appear that Mordechai's grievance is justified.[72]

But in truth, the halacha is like the opinion of Rebbi Akiva, that one's personal survival takes precedence.

Furthermore, while Mordechai felt bad being left alone, by threatening the officer that he must take all of us, we would have gained nothing and would have worsened the situation. We would have remained a group of three and our acceptance into a partisan group would have been more unlikely.

I am grateful that in his book, that not only does Mordechai not malign me in any way, but rather the opposite is true. He often finds reasons to praise me.

---

71 מבעי ליה לכדתניא שנים שהיו מהלכין בדרך
וביד אחד מהן קיתון של מים אם שותין
שניהם מתים ואם שותה אחד מהן מגיע
לישוב דרש בן פטורא מוטב שישתו שניהם
וימותו ואל יראה אחד מהם במיתתו של
חבירו עד שבא ר' עקיבא ולימד וחי אחיך
עמך חייך קודמים לחיי חבירך

72 The Gemara (Talmud) presents a case where two men are travelling on the road in a dry, desolate place, and one of them has a flask of water in hand. If both drink, both will die, because there is not enough water for both of them. If one of them drinks, he will be able to live to reach the settled area.

—EDITOR

95

For example, on page 88, he writes, "It was the eve of Yom Kippur when we arrived exhausted and broken in spirit to the village Andreyovka. How did we know it was Yom Kippur? Because as long as Grainom Lazewnik was with us, we did not have to concern ourselves with the calendar. We were confident in his ability to keep track of the holidays. In all our wanderings we never saw him eat anything non-kosher. He was scrupulous in his observance of mitzvos. Considering the circumstances his behavior required great courage, fortitude and self-sacrifice."

On page 89 he continues, "The partisans asked for help in sawing some logs. We all came forward except for Grainom. He refused because it was Shabbos. They all looked at him in wonderment and curiosity. From which planet did this strange creature fall? They tried arguing with him and then they insulted him, as the partisans knew how, but he remained steadfast. On Shabbos he would not work. It amazed us that he did not pay with his life for this refusal."

13.

LIFE AS A
PARTISAN

NOVEMBER 1942–
SUMMER, 1944

FROM THE TIME WE WERE ACCEPTED INTO THE partisan group, my spiritual and physical life became a bit easier.

While wandering the forests, our existence had been threatened, with every single moment holding potential danger. Now, the danger was diminished, except for when we went on missions against the Germans.

From the winter of 1942 until the summer of 1944, I had more time to quench my spiritual thirst by davening and saying Tehillim.

When the Germans killed the inhabitants of Lenin, they temporarily left alive 28 citizens who had talents or professional skills which the Germans considered important to them. My sister Faygel was among them. Like my brother Moshe, she was an expert photographer.

In mid-September, about a month after the escape from

Hanzovitch, they were rescued when the partisans attacked the Germans that were stationed in Lenin. My sister now joined these partisans. There were some men from Lenin in the group who had joined after the escape from Hanzovitch.

Although they were not far from where I was stationed, I hesitated to visit them. I felt I should always be available to help protect our camp in case of attack, and be ready to leave on a sabotage mission whenever the commander organized one. I did not feel it correct to request leave in order to visit my brother and sister. They were less restricted, and managed to visit me every so often.

Moshe recovered a German parachute made of cotton, a khaki material, and hired a tailor to sew me a suit. I was pleased because I could be certain that the parachute did not contain wool and so the suit was not shatnez,[73] unlike the locally-made garments that had the mixture of woolen material with linen stitching.

When they visited, I would encourage them not to lose

---

[73] Any mixture of wool and linen, which the Torah forbids a Jew to wear. More than simply an interesting moment, Rav Grainom recounts his acquisition of a suit that is certified free of shatnez as another subtle miracle that helped him fortify himself physically and spiritually in his journey. −EDITOR

hope, telling them that I was sure the Jewish people and our Torah would survive, and even flourish, in the future. "One who teaches, learns," is a common saying. As much as I encouraged them, in the process, I fortified myself.

Being able to discern the many revealed and hidden miracles that Hashem wrought on my behalf, helped me to preserve my courage.

I often remembered the Midrash that relates a parable regarding a Jewish man travelling with a number of barrels of wine. One barrel went astray into a neighborhood of non-Jews.[74] The man said, "Let me leave these wagons here, in this public place where non-Jews are not to be found, and quickly go into this non-Jewish area to rescue the wine, before it is contaminated by the gentiles." (Bereishis Rabbah 86.5).[75]

---

74 Jewish law forbids drinking wine that has been touched by a gentile.

–EDITOR

75 ה ויהי ה' את יוסף . ``הא עם שאר השבטים לאו .
אמר רבי יודן לבהמי שהיה לפניו י"ב בהמות
טעונות יין . נכנסה אחת מהם לחנותו של נכרי . הניח
י"א והלך לו אחריה . אמרו לו מה אתה מניח י"א והולך
לך אחרי האחת . אמר להם אלו ברשות הרבים הם
ואיני חושש להן שמא יעשה יין נסך . כך אלו גדולים
וברשות אביהם אבל זה שהוא קטן וברשות עצמו לפיכך
ויהי ה' את יוסף .

Being alone amongst many gentiles, I felt that Hashem was guarding his lone Jew in this spiritually barren and alien environment.

As I continued to try and maintain my spiritual life, the non-Jews continued to guard me physically.

One day, as we prepared our equipment for an operation, the officer in charge ordered me to remain in the camp. I was embarrassed, but said to myself, "This, too, shall be for the good," and accepted the order without complaining.

It turned out that the mission was a very dangerous one. That officer himself, and two others, were killed.

It is quite likely that the commander did not trust his men. He knew that if the battle was a heated one, it would be an opportunity for someone to shoot the lone Jew in the group and claim it was an enemy bullet or an accident.

The partisan officers had difficulty trusting their men because some had been German prisoners in the early part of the war, where they had volunteered to work for the Germans. Later, a group of about twenty was organized, and they entered the forests bringing arms and explosives.

During one mission to blow up a railroad track, our leader,

as well as several others, changed sides twice![76] From the Russian army, to the Germans, and back to the partisans.

I was not aware of how precarious my situation was and how untrustworthy my "colleagues" were until I heard the leader call out to one of them, "Why are you positioning yourself there?" (behind me), "You can't aim well from there!"

After a stream of "blessings" he added, "Why, you coward, you would sooner shoot at one of us than at the enemy!"

"A thief knows his thievery," (Bava Metzia 84a),[77] and can recognize the plans of another thief.

By adding this last sentence, the leader was letting me know with whom I needed to be careful.

At that moment I said, "In the way that I go, they have hidden a snare for me . . . You are my shelter, my share in the land of the living." (Tehillim 142.4-6).[78]

---

76 Presumably, Rav Grainom means to say here that one mission on which he was assigned was led and staffed by several men who had had changed sides during the course of World War II, twice, starting with service in the Russian army, then serving with the Germans, lastly joining the partisans. —EDITOR

77 לסטאה בלסטיותיה

78 בְּאֹרַח־זוּ אֲהַלֵּךְ טָמְנוּ פַח לִי
אַתָּה מַחְסִי, חֶלְקִי בְּאֶרֶץ הַחַיִּים

"Be my secure place to live where I can always rest, You have commanded that I be saved. You are my rock and my fortress." (Tehillim 71.3).[79]

After the operation, we had a meeting to assess the effort. The officer praised me for bravery, and publicly denigrated the "coward" of the unit.

I said quietly, "It is good to give thanks to You, Hashem, and to sing praises to Your name, Most High." (Tehillim 92.2).[80] I can discern those that plot against me, "My eyes see the desire of my enemies. My ears hear the wicked that rise up against me." (Tehillim 92.12).[81]

As I reflect back and review these events, I feel utter astonishment. Could it really have been that my life had been preserved by a brutal and murderous turncoat? Who could say how many men, women, and children he'd killed?

---

79 הֱיֵה לִי לְצוּר מָעוֹן לָבוֹא תָּמִיד צִוִּיתָ לְהוֹשִׁיעֵנִי, כִּי־סַלְעִי וּמְצוּדָתִי אָתָּה

80 טוֹב לְהֹדוֹת לַ ה', וּלְזַמֵּר לְשִׁמְךָ עֶלְיוֹן

81 וַתַּבֵּט עֵינִי בְּשׁוּרָי, בַּקָּמִים עָלַי מְרֵעִים תִּשְׁמַעְנָה אָזְנָי

"And kings shall be your nursing fathers," (Yeshaya 49.23).[82]
An officer who had served the Nazis protected me! "How great
are Your works, Hashem, very deep are Your thoughts!" (Tehillim 92.6).[83]

---

82 וְהָיוּ מְלָכִים אֹמְנַיִךְ וְשָׂרוֹתֵיהֶם מֵינִיקֹתָיִךְ

83 מַה־גָּדְלוּ מַעֲשֶׂיךָ ה' , מְאֹד עָמְקוּ
מַחְשְׁבֹתֶיךָ :

14.

PASSOVER AS
A SHEPHERD

SPRING, 1944

SHORTLY BEFORE PESACH 1944, THE COMmander ordered me to leave my rifle at the base and to accompany a local partisan to another area. I was quite surprised at this unusual development.

My companion was familiar with the terrain, and he led the way across a large and barely passable swamp.

Our destination was an elevated, partially-wooded pasture, surrounded on all sides by dense swamps. I was introduced to the commissar, who explained what my job was to be for the next two weeks.

A herd of cows was secretly kept there, in case food from other sources was unavailable for the partisans. The shepherd's assistant had to leave, and I was his replacement for two weeks.

A day after Pesach, the assistant returned. What good fortune! For the duration of the holiday I did not have to eat any chametz (leavened bread).[84] During those two weeks, I never experienced hunger, as I drank a quart of fresh milk each morning and evening.

I considered myself fortunate for not having to eat chametz, but there was an added bonus. I had time to rest and recover my strength. I didn't know it yet, but the most difficult period of my refugee period was about to begin.

During these two weeks, I recited the blessing, "Blessed be He, Who girds Yisroel with strength,"[85] with special intent.[86] The many hours a day spent sitting in the grass under the blue spring sky inspired me, and brought the verse, "Hashem is my Shepherd, I do not want. He lets me lie down in lush pastures, He leads me by still waters," (Tehillim 23.1-2)[87] constantly on my lips.

---

84   The Torah forbids a Jew to eat anything containing chametz, leavening, for the week-long period of Pesach. (Shmos 13.3, 7).   —EDITOR

85   בָּרוּךְ אַתָּה יְיָ אֱלֹקֵינוּ מֶלֶךְ הָעוֹלָם אוֹזֵר יִשְׂרָאֵל בִּגְבוּרָה

86   This blessing is part of "Bircas Ha Shachar," a set of blessings recited after awakening in the morning which acknowledges the goodness of the Creator, transforming a person from the passivity of sleep to activity.   —EDITOR

87   ה' רֹעִי לֹא אֶחְסָר: בִּנְאוֹת דֶּשֶׁא יַרְבִּיצֵנִי, עַל־מֵי מְנֻחוֹת יְנַהֲלֵנִי

In my situation, the "still waters" flowed with sweet milk. Milk that revived my body and spirit, like manna from the Heavens. "He restores my soul, He leads me on paths of righteousness for the sake of His name." (Tehillim 23.3).[88]

I felt His grace in this amazing and wonderous situation; for the Pesach holiday I was given responsibilities that enabled me to avoid eating any chametz! "How shall a young man improve his ways? By heeding Your word."[89] (Tehillim 119.9).[90]

What merit did I have, being so young and ignorant, to be "led on a righteous path" and not have to transgress the law of Pesach? "Your rod and Your staff, they comfort me." (Tehillim 23.4).[91] As much as the rod hurts, and in a time when the rod smites so indiscriminately and so forcefully, still, a person can

---

[88] נַפְשִׁי יְשׁוֹבֵב, יַנְחֵנִי בְמַעְגְּלֵי־צֶדֶק לְמַעַן שְׁמוֹ

[89] Here Rav Grainom thanks the Almighty for the ability to "improve his ways" by "heeding His word." That is, he sees Divine providence in the opportunity to be meticulous in the commandment to avoid eating chometz on Pesach. This demonstrates the principle, "the reward for a mitzvah is a mitzvah," (Avos 4.2) that is, from Heaven, help comes to one who keeps a mitzvah, to do another mitzvah (Rav Ovadiah of Bartenura).   –EDITOR

[90] בַּמֶּה יְזַכֶּה־נַּעַר אֶת־אָרְחוֹ לִשְׁמֹר כִּדְבָרֶךָ

[91] שִׁבְטְךָ וּמִשְׁעַנְתֶּךָ הֵמָּה יְנַחֲמֻנִי

take comfort, "You prepare a table before me," in spite of the overhanging rod. (Tehillim 23.5). [92]

When I returned to the base, our brigade was placed on special alert. The summer of 1944 was approaching, and the German army was in retreat.

The cities and smaller towns, even the forests, were crowded with Germans, as they retraced their steps backwards out of Russia and part of what had been Poland.

The strongholds established by the partisans in the countryside were now threatened.

Our commander had us move to the small, dry hilltops found every so often in the vast swamps. We hoped that the swamps would impede German attack and, perhaps, even discourage them from attacking altogether.

The day of the expected attack arrived.

The atmosphere was tense.

Our arms and equipment were battle-ready.

To everyone's surprise, the day passed and the Germans did not appear. The tension dissipated.

What happened?

---

[92] תַּעֲרֹךְ לְפָנַי שֻׁלְחָן נֶגֶד צֹרְרָי

The Germans had planned to surround and attack the entire area where the partisans camped. At the last moment, a cable arrived, ordering an immediate evacuation. The German army was to hurry westward, out of Russia, toward Germany and France, at once.

On June 6, American and British armies had landed on the beaches of Normandy, France. The great counter-attack by the Allies to liberate Europe was underway.

For the past three years, we had been under Nazi occupation. Day to day, hour to hour, our lives hung in the balance. Those last few days waiting for the attack were the most frightening of all.

"You bring a man to the point of his returning into dust." (Tehillim 90.3).[93] Only to the edge of despair, does Hashem bring us.

When our fate seemed most bleak and hopeless, Hashem's redemption arrived. How important it is to learn not to lose faith. "Even if a sharp sword is resting at a man's neck, he should not refrain from seeking Divine mercy." (Berachos 10a).[94]

---

93 תָּשֵׁב אֱנוֹשׁ עַד־דַּכָּא

94 אפי' חרב חדה מונחת על צוארו של אדם
אל ימנע עצמו מן הרחמים

The danger confronting us passed, as the Germans hastened to leave.

After the German retreat, some of the partisans returned to their hometowns and established governing bodies. My group entered Luban. Others went to Starobin, Slutsk, Pinsk and Minsk. The rest of us, myself included, were dispatched to the Russian army.

My sister Faygel came to Luban, to tell me that she had arranged for me to serve on the Pinsk city council. I had left Luban the day before she arrived. She returned to Pinsk, greatly disappointed about not finding me.

However, this was one more episode in which I was led in the right direction from Heaven.

Going to serve on the front entailed great physical danger. From a halachic standpoint, I may have been obligated to accept the job with the communist regime. This would have placed me in a situation of internal conflict, regarding desecrating the Shabbos, working conditions being what they were.[95]

---

95 Accepting an appointment to the city council in Soviet-controlled Pinsk would have put Rav Grainom in a situation where he felt certain he would be forced to desecrate the Shabbos. This certain spiritual danger, in his later estimation, may have been worse than the very real threat of physical danger posed by joining the front lines of battle. Rav Grainom expresses gratitude to the

The dilemma and quandary of making such a decision was beyond my emotional abilities at the time. (Having no occupation at all was totally not a viable option in the "worker's paradise.")[96]

After returning safely from the front, when I learned from my sister what had transpired, I said to myself, "I will call upon Hashem, most High, to Hashem, Who fulfills for me." (Tehillim 57.3),[97] "The Powerful One, Who girds me with strength and Who made my way perfect." (Tehillim 18.33).[98]

Almighty here for sparing him from having to make such a difficult choice between two opposite dangers.   –EDITOR

96   A sarcastic reference to the propaganda of the U.S.S.R. which claimed that communism made it an ideal state for the working class. The Soviet government required all citizens to be employed, and Torah study was not recognized as a profession.   –EDITOR

97   אֶקְרָא לֵאלֹקִים עֶלְיוֹן, לָקֵל גֹּמֵר עָלָי

98   הָקֵל הַמְאַזְּרֵנִי חָיִל, וַיִּתֵּן תָּמִים דַּרְכִּי

15.

IN THE
RUSSIAN ARMY

SUMMER, 1944

I SPENT THE SUMMER OF 1944 IN TRAINING FOR the Russian army.

Each day, more and more soldiers joined our ranks. Most were either youngsters, aged 18, 19, or older fellows of 45-50, from the Siberia region. Most men between the ages of 20 and 45 had already been drafted into the Russian army. I was an exception because I was from the West, eastern Poland.

One day, a "landsman," Mordechai Migdalovitch, arrived. (He now lives in Ramat Eliyahu, Rishon LeTzion).

"How precious to me are the friends of Hashem." (Tehillim 139.17, according to Rashi).[99] I was overjoyed to have a Yid to share my lot with. How much better to have an ally, than to be alone.

---

99 וְלִי מַה־יָּקְרוּ רֵעֶיךָ קל

I thought to myself, "Two are better than one, because they have a better reward for their labor." (Koheles 4.9).[100]

Mordechai suffered greatly from pangs of hunger. His large, muscular physique demanded more food than it received. He asked me to give him my bowl, so he could receive an extra portion. Since anyway, I would not partake of cooked food, at least another Jew could benefit from my rations.

I discouraged him from doing so.

However, one day he came and boasted about his will-power. He said that he did not eat the meat that day because it was horse meat. The meat of a horse killed the previous day was put into the pot.

I explained to him that horse meat is no more forbidden to us, than meat of a kosher animal not ritually slaughtered.[101] I therefore suggested that I'd give him my bowl so that he could have an extra portion, if he would promise to eat only the soup

---

100 טוֹבִים הַשְּׁנַיִם מִן־הָאֶחָד אֲשֶׁר יֵשׁ־לָהֶם שָׂכָר טוֹב בַּעֲמָלָם

101 The Torah text references the tradition received by Moshe on Mount Sinai of slaughter of a kosher animal. The only method of slaughter permitted for a Jewish person to eat is called shechita. A single slice of the jugular immediately induces unconsciousness and inflicts the minimum amount of pain to the animal. —EDITOR

and vegetables, but not the meat itself, since eating a food cooked with non-kosher meat is not as bad as eating the meat itself.

Mordechai agreed.

In the evenings, while I retreated to a quiet corner, under the trees, to pray and sleep, he would work in the kitchen, in order to earn a few extra mouthfuls of food.

One evening, he told me that, while working there, he heard volunteers were being sought for an officers training program.

He was not enthusiastic about the idea. He reminded me that, when the war ended, it would be far more difficult for an officer to get an exit visa and leave Communist Russia.

I felt differently. We were three miles from the front lines, and within a day or two, would be in battle.

What could be more dangerous than this? "Deal with each problem at its time." (Berachos 9b).[102] When it is time to leave Russia, Hashem will show a way out. "Hashem possesses many messengers." (Rashi to Shmos 16.32).[103]

I convinced him to go immediately, and sign both of us up for the course.

---

[102] רבש"ע דיה לצרה בשעתה

[103] הַרְבֵּה שְׁלוּחִין יֵשׁ לוֹ לַמָּקוֹס

Late that evening, we were issued live ammunition. Until then, we practiced shooting using wooden "bullets."

At two in the morning, we were awakened and lined up.

Before beginning the march to the battlefield, the sergeant quietly excused eight soldiers, including Mordechai and myself. We waited on the side. The other soldiers left to the front nearby.

The first order we received was to go to a point, off in the distance. One of the eight was appointed leader. It was a command post of the Russian army, and we were told to guard it.

(We were never trained to be officers. I believe that their request for volunteers to become officers was a way for them to recruit guards whom they could more readily trust for this important assignment.)

That afternoon, two wounded soldiers passed by on their way to the infirmary. They were the only survivors from the entire group who had left late last night to engage the Germans on Hill Number 86, as it was designated on the map.

"To Him, Who alone performs great wonders, for His kindness endures forever." (Tehillim 136.4).[104]

---

104 לְעֹשֵׂה נִפְלָאוֹת גְּדֹלוֹת לְבַדּוֹ,
כִּי לְעוֹלָם חַסְדּוֹ

Sometimes Hashem performs a miracle that is understood only later on, and sometimes not at all. (Nidah 31a).[105]

The next morning, we were sent to the battlefield to load the dead bodies onto trucks. The pile of corpses got so high that I did not have strength to throw any more bodies to the top without them rolling off to the ground.

My partner turned to me and said, "There are no Jews among these corpses. The Jews are in Moscow, standing in line to receive sugar rations."

"Don't talk to him that way," answered a worker from another truck. "Go to Moscow and tell them your complaints, if you care to, but meanwhile, he is here putting his life on the line with the rest of us—so why are you barking at him?"

Everyone was silent, though I quietly whispered, "You Hashem, are a protecting shield on my behalf, my Honor, and the One Who lifts my head." (Tehillim 3.4).[106] "My G-d, for You have struck all my enemies on the cheek, the teeth of the wicked You have broken." (Tehillim 3.8).[107]

---

105 אפילו בעל הנם אינו מכיר בנסו

106 וְאַתָּה ה' מָגֵן בַּעֲדִי, כְּבוֹדִי וּמֵרִים רֹאשִׁי

107 אֱלֹקַי כִּי־הִכִּיתָ אֶת־כָּל־אֹיְבַי לֶחִי, שִׁנֵּי רְשָׁעִים שִׁבַּרְתָּ

That night, before I went to sleep, I reflected on how Mordechai and I had been but a short step from death. If Mordechai had not overheard the request for volunteers, we might not have been saved. I avoided the company of my comrades as much as possible, and would not have known of the officers course. "Hashem protects the simple, I was brought low and He saved me." (Tehillim 116.6).[108]

Regarding my decision, I said, "I will bless Hashem, Who has given me counsel, my reins also admonish me in the night." (Tehillim 16.7).[109] "You will not commit my soul to the grave, nor will you let Your holy one to see the pit." (Tehillim 16.10).[110]

---

[108] שֹׁמֵר פְּתָאיִם ה' , דַּלֹּתִי וְלִי יְהוֹשִׁיעַ

[109] אֲבָרֵךְ אֶת־ ה' אֲשֶׁר יְעָצָנִי, אַף־לֵילוֹת יִסְּרוּנִי כִלְיוֹתָי

[110] כִּי לֹא־תַעֲזֹב נַפְשִׁי לִשְׁאוֹל, לֹא־תִתֵּן חֲסִידְךָ לִרְאוֹת שָׁחַת

16.

YOM KIPPUR, IN THE RUSSIAN ARMY

OCTOBER 1944

OUR TERM OF GUARD DUTY AMOUNTED TO spending a number of weeks training, during the day, and digging large, house-sized holes in the ground at night.

Why this was necessary, we did not know, although the air was rife with rumors. (One explanation, was that it was meant to disguise the headquarters of the generals.)

I suffered terribly from lack of sleep. I reproached myself, "If I was worthy, I'd go sleepless and spend the nights learning Torah. Since I did not spend my nights learning, I must now spend them digging holes."

Yom Kippur 1944 arrived.

I mused to myself, "If only it was possible to explain that I have a religious obligation not to eat today. How can I be expected to work on a fast day?"

Understanding the impossibility of broaching the subject,

I decided to take matters into my own hands. Yom Kippur morning, I remained on the pile of straw where I slept.

"I am tired, absolutely exhausted, I cannot get up this morning," I explained.

I was left alone. Except for a few prayers and mishnayos[111] that I recited from memory, I spent the entire day sleeping. A guard assigned to the barracks did not notice me praying, as he spent most of his time outside, only occasionally coming in.

Toward evening, the soldiers returned from training exercises. The first soldier to enter the barracks immediately began to insult me.

"Look at this sneaky Jew, who managed to avoid working today," he spouted.

"Not true," the guard answered him, "I've been keeping an eye on him, and I can testify that not a morsel of food entered his mouth all day."

The soldiers decided to leave me be.

---

[111] The Mishna is the framework of the Oral Law, containing authoritative rulings for the entire corpus of "halacha," the general term for the fulfillment of the commandments of the Torah. The Mishna is divided into six sedorim (orders) composed of individual masechtos (volumes) which are, in turn, divided into perokim (chapters) broken down into individual groups of rulings, known as mishnayos. —EDITOR

They let me rest, and justified it by saying, "A person who cannot eat, cannot work."

Softly, I recited to myself, "When a man's ways please Hashem, even his enemies will make peace with him." (Mishlei 16.7).[112]

---

112 בִּרְצוֹת ה' דַּרְכֵי־אִישׁ גַּם־אוֹיְבָיו יַשְׁלִם אִתּוֹ

17.

WOUNDED ON THE FRONT LINE

WINTER, 1945

INEVITABLY, THE DAY CAME WHEN I WAS SENT to the front line.

The Germans sporadically shelled our positions. A number of times, I reached out of my trench to touch hot pieces of metal shrapnel that had just exploded around me.[113]

[ ]

ON JANUARY 16, 1945, WE BEGAN THE ATTACK THAT continued until the Germans surrendered.

[ ]

THERE WAS INCESSANT WHISTLING OF BOMBS coupled with earth tremors. It felt as if the entire earth was roaring.

---

113 Apparently, while he was attempting to climb up out of the trench. Rav Grainom is showing how deep into the battle his position was.   –EDITOR

With the first light of dawn, we were ordered out of the trenches, to press forward.

We passed the empty trenches of the retreating Germans.

Around noontime, a small explosive went off under my right foot.

The front half of my boot was completely destroyed, pulverized into dust. To the surprise of everyone, the cloth wrapped around my foot to serve as a sock was untouched, except for a small tear of the side of my big toe. The cut was smeared with black soot from the explosive. Half my toe was separated from the bone, and it remained attached by flesh and skin. The bone itself was broken in half.

I tried to stop the bleeding, using the bandage that was standard issue to all soldiers. I did not want my foot to get infected from the soot, so I left the broken half of my toe outside the bandage.

Unable to stop the bleeding, I had no choice but to include the separated part of my toe inside the bandage.

Later, I learned that this slowed down the healing process.

As a result of this wound, I would spend the rest of the war in medical facilities.

[ ]

WHEN I REACHED THE INFIRMARY, I WAS ORDERED
to empty my pockets and return the uniform.

They promised to forward the contents to the hospital. That
was the last I ever saw of my tefillin. I had kept them with me
throughout the war years.

For three months, I was on a military hospital-train full of
wounded soldiers, travelling to Opah, where a large hospital
was located. During the Czar's reign, political prisoners were
exiled to Opah. It was 900 miles east from Moscow, and more
than 1200 miles from where I was wounded.

In one car, emergency surgery was performed.[114] During
these three months, I did not receive any medical attention.
Even at the hospital in Opah, I had a long wait until I received
medical attention.

---

114 It seems Rav Grainom is setting the stage for his later reflections on Divine Providence. Emergency surgery could have been performed even in this
makeshift train hospital. Had his injury been adequately treated, he would have
been fit to be sent back to the front lines. It was the lengthy duration of his re-
cuperation that delayed his return to battle until the war had ended.

–EDITOR

When, at last, the surgeon operated, it was without anesthesia.

I heard the sound of metal particles falling to the floor, as the surgeon cleaned the broken bone.

"His soul was restrained by metal," (Tehillim 105.18)[115] had come to be.[116]

After cleaning the wound, the surgeon noticed that only a small part of the bone remained.

For this reason, or perhaps for another that I am unaware of, he said to his colleagues, "We have no choice, we have to amputate the toe."

"Please," I said. "I do not have the strength to bear any more."

He respected my wish, and rebandaged my toe.

[‫נ‬]

A WHILE LATER, WHEN MAKING HIS ROUNDS WITH a group of younger doctors, he proudly showed them my toe

---

115 עִנּוּ בַכֶּבֶל רגליו בַּרְזֶל בָּאָה נַפְשׁוֹ

116 As Rav Grainom explained earlier (pg. 12), this was the second verse that came to his mind when he awoke, early in the morning before he received the notice ordering him to report for military duty with the Polish army at the outbreak of the war. —EDITOR

and said, "I would never have believed that this wound would heal as well as it did, and not require further surgery."

Because the bone remained broken and separated, the healing process took much longer, and I did not return to the front.

When I understood this, I said, "The recipient of a miracle is not always aware it's transpiring." (Nidah 31a).[117]

[ב]

ON APRIL 30, 1945, RUSSIAN FORCES ENTERED BERLIN, the capital of Germany, and eight days later, all German resistance ceased.

Still, Russian soldiers who recuperated returned to active duty. The rumor circulating was that they would be sent to the far east to fight Japan. (The atom bomb was dropped months later, in August.)

I was feeling weary, not only because I did not want to be a soldier any longer, but also from the strain of being in the company of non-Jews without a friend, tefillin or Torah. I had no idea how long it would be until I would be discharged.

I prayed, "Save me, Almighty, the waters around me have

אפילו בעל הנם אינו מכיר בנסו 117

risen dangerously high." (Tehillim 69.2).[118] I felt my soul's strength dissipating, and my emotional fortitude ebbing.

As my physical state improved, my spiritual needs required more attention.

I heard that an old rabbi from Kiev was in the city. With my bandaged foot, I hobbled over to pay him a visit.

"I have no tefillin for you," he said.

"Perhaps you have a sefer,[119] a scholarly book, to lend me?" I asked.

At that moment, a fifty or sixty-year old woman came into the room from the nearby kitchen. Surely, she overheard the conversation. She joined us at the table.

"This is my daughter," he introduced. And then, with an affected pride, he added, "She is a member of the Communist party."

I immediately understood that I should not speak in her presence.[120] I bid them farewell and returned to the hospital.

I approached my doctor, and asked if it was possible to be

---

118 הוֹשִׁיעֵנִי אֱלֹקִים כִּי בָאוּ מַיִם עַד־נָפֶשׁ

119 Hebrew word for "book," used to refer to a text of Torah matters.
—EDITOR

120 Officially an atheistic state, the USSR forbade the practice of any religion whatsoever. —EDITOR

transferred to my hometown area, Minsk, the capital of White Russia.

"If you can get a letter of admission to the hospital there, you can go," he answered, matter-of-factly.

At once, I found some blank paper and wrote to my brother Moshe. I assumed he was in Minsk, because it is the capital of White Russia, and I thought the partisans would choose it as their headquarters.

I had no specific address, so I wrote, "Moshe Lazevnik– Minsk."

To my amazement, only two weeks later, I received his reply! He sent five hundred rubles and a letter from the local hospital stating that they had room for me.

My doctor signed a release form, and gave me my medical file, although I was almost completely recovered. Had I remained under his care, it was only a matter of days before he would remove my bandages and release me from the hospital.

I knew that a Jewish heart beat in his chest, though he never gave the slightest hint. On occasion, the gentiles would joke about this Jewish doctor's fate, who had been sent to serve here from afar, into exile.

18.

ON MY
WAY HOME

SPRING–SUMMER, 1945

I LEFT THE HOSPITAL AND WENT TO THE TRAIN station.

I was beside myself with gratitude. "What can I repay Hashem, for all His beneficence toward me? A cup of salvation I will lift up, and the name of Hashem I will call out." (Tehillim 116.12-13).[121]

Again I remembered the teaching of the Midrash, how Hashem protects His "wine" so that it will not become contaminated.

"And Hashem was with Yosef." (Bereishis 39.2).[122] Why with Yosef, more than with his brothers? Because the brothers

---

מָה־אָשִׁיב לַ ה' כָּל־תַּגְמוּלוֹהִי עָלָי : כּוֹס־יְשׁוּעוֹת אֶשָּׂא, 121
וּבְשֵׁם ה' אֶקְרָא

וַיְהִי ה' אֶת־יוֹסֵף 122

were at home with their father, while Yosef was alone in a foreign environment. (Bereishis Rabbah ch. 86).[123]

My train stopped in Moscow, and while taking a stroll, I saw a large sign that read: "Organization of Polish Patriots."

Upon entering, a Jewish man led me from one completely empty room to the next. Finally, he opened a door, and sitting behind a large desk was Rabbi Eliezer Sorotskin (now living in Eretz Yisroel), son of the famed Rabbi Zalman Sorotskin of Lutsk.[124]

I introduced myself as a yeshiva student in the "Red" (Russian) army.

---

123   ה וַיְהִי ה' אֶת יוֹסֵף .

הוא עם שאר השבטים לאו . כך אלו גדולים
וברשות אביהם אבל זה שהוא קטן וברשות עצמו לפיכך
ויהי ה' את יוסף .

124   The descriptions of his post-war travels are not meant to be mere biography; Rav Grainom has stated in the Introduction to this book, that the purpose of this book was to record the praise of the Almighty for His miracles and kindness, not to write his own life story. That is why discussions of his own encounters with illustrious Torah scholars in the yeshivos of Europe are absent from this book. The purpose of this chapter, it appears, is to detail how the Almighty continued to provide for Rav Grainom's needs, following the war, while a less refined person might simply attribute these fortunate circumstances to human philanthropy or community activism.   —EDITOR

Rav Sorotskin interrupted me, and called to the Jewish man who was waiting by the door, "Give him a set of clothes."

I quietly followed him to a room that was full of all types of garments and uniforms that apparently had been sent from England or America. I chose a suit and left.

I then visited the famous Moskwa shul, where I met Rabbi Shlaifer, the official Chief Rabbi of the former Soviet Union. He told me I could obtain books in Malachuvkah, a suburb of Moscow.

I went there, and filled a sack full of seforim.

Later, I left them in Lodz, when I realized I had too much to carry, thinking to myself, wherever there will be a Jewish community, there will be a Shas and Poskim.[125]

The next day, when I met Rabbi Shlaifer in the shul, he

---

[125] The term "Shas" refers to either the complete Mishnayos (as an abbreviation of "Shisha Sidre," the Six Orders of the Mishnah) or, more commonly, as a reference to the entire Gemara, or Talmud. The authoritative rulings on the practical application of Torah law to contemporary questions is known as "poskim." Here, Rav Grainom refers to "Shas and poskim" in a colloquial sense of finding a study hall that has a complete set of all the volumes of the Gemara and the later authorities. A reader can almost sense the resignation Rav Grainom felt, having to abandon a bag filled with scholarly books, which he filled in his excitement after years away from learning, only to find it too heavy to carry in his travels. —EDITOR

asked me if I had taken a manuscript that was among the seforim.

I answered that I had not.

He seemed disappointed to hear this, but did not pursue the subject further.

All the remaining seforim, including the manuscript, were destroyed by fire a few years later.

I believe that Rabbi Shlaifer's intention was that I should take the manuscript to the free world. I was apprehensive and thought it risky to take it. In retrospect, I regret not taking it.[126]

When I met Rabbi Sorotskin[127] in shul, he suggested that when I reached Pinsk (the Jewish metropolis near my hometown Lenin) I should request an official travel pass to Moscow

---

126 These pangs of regret may have later spurred Rav Grainom to smuggle a different manuscript, which was an explanation of the Rif (an early commentator on the Gemara), out of the USSR when he left for America. When he published that commentary to the Rif, Rav Grainom took the opportunity to publicize the miracles that took place which allowed him make this work of scholarship available to others. He appended as an afterward "Persumei Nesei" in Hebrew, translated as "Personal Miracles", this book which we call, "Guarded from Above." —EDITOR

127 Apparently this is the same Rav Eliezer Sorotskin who issued Rav Grainom a new suit of clothes when Rav Grainom visited the building advertised as "Organization of Polish Patriots" recounted earlier in this chapter. —EDITOR

to receive a Torah scroll from him.[128] All he asked in return was that I bring him news regarding Pinsk.

I left Moscow and journeyed to Minsk, 420 miles to the west. I met with my brother Moshe, and the next day, I continued on to Pinsk, 140 miles to the southwest.

The destruction of this Jewish city was complete. Not one Jewish soul of the pre-war population was there.

Lying in heaps on the streets were Jewish books, including one written by Rabbi Sorotskin's uncle, Rabbi Aharon Walkin. It was printed before the war, but never distributed.

I was astonished to find that amidst all the chaos and destruction, a minyan[129] had been formed in a small synagogue. They even had a Torah scroll. Some older Russian Jews had brought it with them when they recently came to Pinsk, to be reunited with their children and grandchildren.

The younger generation had come to rebuild and reorganize

---

128 That is to say, when Rav Sorotskin learned Rav Grainom was planning to travel from Moscow to Pinsk, he offered to give Rav Grainom a Torah scroll upon his return if Rav Grainom brought back word as to the news in Pinsk. A Torah scroll is painstakingly handwritten and is a very expensive, as well as holy, item.   –EDITOR

129 A group of ten Jewish men above the age of bar mitzvah, gathered for prayer, the minimum number to be considered a group representing the Jewish people.   –EDITOR

the city's life, and brought their parents with them. "See how this nation is Your people." (Shmos 33.13).[130] "The Eternal One of Yisroel will not lie." (Shmuel 1 15.29).[131] Hashem will not "change His mind" about the eternal existence of the Jewish people.

Seeing is greater than hearing. Seeing the complete destruction of Pinsk, where not one survivor existed, neither from Pinsk, nor from neighboring Karlin, was heartbreaking.

I felt restless, and decided to forget about travelling back to Rabbi Sorotskin.

My sister and her husband, Moshe Shulman, escorted me and helped me carry the sack of seforim to the train.

I traveled to Lodz, 275 miles to the west of Pinsk. There I found a bais medresh and a bais din (rabbinical court), organized by a rabbi from Lodz. A few yeshiva students were learning there.

I decided to stay until after the Sukkos holiday. "I am a friend to all those that fear You." (Tehillim 119.63).[132]

---

130 וּרְאֵה כִּי עַמְּךָ הַגּוֹי הַזֶּה

131 וְגַם נֵצַח יִשְׂרָאֵל לֹא יְשַׁקֵּר וְלֹא יִנָּחֵם
כִּי לֹא אָדָם הוּא לְהִנָּחֵם

132 חָבֵר אָנִי לְכָל־אֲשֶׁר יְרֵאוּךָ

During Rosh Hashanah and Yom Kippur, I could not help but remember the High Holidays of 1942 when we prayed in the home of our neighbor Yekusial (Cusha) Galenson. Some of his sons were killed when they were captured together with our neighbor Yerachmiel Dvorin.

"You have covered Yourself with a cloud, so that our prayers could not pass through. You have covered with anger and pursued us, You have slain and not pitied." (Eicha 3.44, 43).[133]

Or, perhaps due to their successful repentance and prayers, they were chosen to represent us and die a martyr's death.

Just before Sukkos, my sister and her husband Moshe Shulman arrived.

After the holiday, we travelled together to Landsberg, Germany, where they joined other partisans.

I continued on to Salzheim, where the righteous Rabbi Gershon Leibman had invited me to head a group of ten of his senior students, and open a yeshiva in the American zone, with the support of the Vaad Hatzolah of New York. New students arrived daily.

---

133   סַכּוֹתָה בֶעָנָן לָךְ מֵעֲבוֹר תְּפִלָּה

חָמָלְתָּ   לֹא   הָרַגְתָּ   וַתִּרְדְּפֵנוּ   בְאַף   סַכּוֹתָה

Rav Gershon and his students had been exiled from Vilna to several labor and extermination camps, including Bergen Belsen. Only ten of his students managed to stay with him until their liberation by the British army.

One student, Dovid'l, had been in the gas chamber, when a Nazi opened the door and pulled him out seconds before the gas was released. The Nazi wanted him as a personal servant.[134]

That summer, Reb Gershon married. We all travelled together to Bergen Belsen for the wedding.

When we passed through Frankfurt, I saw it as an opportunity to register for a visa to leave for a country outside of Europe, either Palestine or America.

The clerk asked me where I was born.

I answered, as usual, Poland. But for a reason that I cannot explain, I added that my hometown was now occupied by Russia.

"The thoughts of the heart belong to man, but from

---

134   Rav Grainom recounts a succession of events, from the rapid establishment of yeshivos after the war, the miraculous salvation of his friend, Dovid'l, and the marriage of his mentor, Rav Gershon Leibman, to show the hand of Heaven in helping him and his colleagues renew their lives after the war.

−EDITOR

Hashem come the utterances of the tongue." (Mishlei 16.1).[135] If a person cannot organize his thoughts consciously, he inadvertently has a slip of the tongue that Heaven places in his mouth.

The clerk knew that it was to my benefit to be registered as a refugee from Russia, rather than from Poland, so he wrote on my application, "Russia."

To everyone's surprise, I received a visa to America a few weeks later.

From this experience, my colleagues learned to register as Russian refugees. "I became as an example to many, You were my mighty refuge; let my mouth be filled with Your praise all the day." (Tehillim 71.7-8).[136]

[ב]

ABOUT A YEAR LATER, I WAS IN MY FATHER-IN-law's house, for the first time for a Friday night Shabbos meal.

It amazed me, to recognize the family that I had dreamed

---

135 לְאָדָם מַעַרְכֵי־לֵב וּמֵ ה' מַעֲנֵה לָשׁוֹן

136 כְּמוֹפֵת הָיִיתִי לְרַבִּים, וְאַתָּה מַחֲסִי־עֹז
יִמָּלֵא פִי תְּהִלָּתֶךָ, כָּל־הַיּוֹם תִּפְאַרְתֶּךָ

about, eating their Shabbos meal in the forest.[137]

[ב]

"THE TALL TREES IN THE DREAM REPRESENTED MEN of learning and stature." (Rashi to Berachos 57a).[138]

If, at present, my brothers-in-law were young, they would, in time, be scholars and heads of yeshiva as well.

This dream became reality. I myself became a Rosh Yeshiva in Salzheim, Germany.[139]

Our Sages say, "A person should wait even 22 years for a

---

137 The Editor asked Rav Grainom, when the Rav was at his new bride's house for Shabbos for the first time, did he recognize the faces of his inlaws as the same faces of the family from his dream? "No," Rav Grainom answered, "It was the feeling that was the same." —EDITOR

138 הנכנס לאגם בחלום נעשה ראש ישיבה
ליער נעשה ראש לבני כלה
יער. אילנות גדולים ומינן סמוכים זה לזה
אף זה סימן לראש לתלמידי הרב
והוא ראש לבני כלה שמפרש
לתלמידים שמועתם אחר שעמד
הרב והם מחזרין על שמועתם ויש
תלמידים שלא יבינו בדברי הרב ככל
הצורך וזה מבינה להם:

139 Since the Gemara states that one who enters a forest in his dream will become a Rosh Yeshiva, the head of a Torah academy, Rav Grainom records here how this dream was fulfilled through his leadership of a newly-founded Novardok yeshiva after the war as mentioned above on page 149. —EDITOR

good dream's actualization." (Berachos 55b).[140]

And so it was. In less than twenty-two years, these young students of New York yeshivos became Torah scholars, heads of yeshiva colleges and staunch supporters of every important endeavor of Klal Yisroel.

The Shabbos challah that was eaten by them in the forest symbolized those that will merit to have a place in Olam Habba, the World to Come. (See the siddur of Rav Yaakov Emden).

My prayer, at that time, was "Their share, shall also be mine, and in their lot, shall I share."[141]

With the help of Hashem, I too shall merit my share in the World to Come.

My entreaty to Him is that we may all continue to see, with clarity, the constant guiding hand of Providence.

---

140 א"ר לוי לעולם יצפה אדם לחלום טוב
עד כ"ב שנה

141 During the production of this book, the Editor asked Rav Grainom, that early in the story the Rav says he passed over an opportunity to emigrate to America before the war, because he felt that America was a midbar, a wilderness, a place devoid of Torah. Perhaps his dream of a "table in the wilderness," was a glimpse of Jewish life that would flourish in the wilderness of America? "That was not how I interpreted it at the time," Rav Grainom answered.

—EDITOR